Company's Coming ®

LUNCHES

by
Jean Paré

Cover Photo

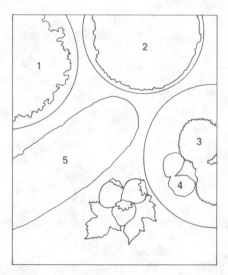

LUNCHES

Second Printing April, 1992

I.S.B.N. 1-895455-00-6

Published and Distributed by
Company's Coming Publishing Limited
Box 8037, Station "F"
Edmonton, Alberta, Canada
T6H 4N9

Printed in Canada

Cookbooks in the Company's Coming series by Jean Paré:

English Hard Cover Title

JEAN PARÉ'S FAVORITES
VOLUME ONE

English Soft Cover Titles

150 DELICIOUS SQUARES

CASSEROLES

MUFFINS & MORE

SALADS

APPETIZERS

DESSERTS

SOUPS & SANDWICHES

HOLIDAY ENTERTAINING

COOKIES

VEGETABLES

MAIN COURSES

PASTA

CAKES

BARBECUES

DINNERS OF THE WORLD

LUNCHES

PIES (September, 1992)

Cookbooks in the Jean Paré series:

French Soft Cover Titles

150 DÉLICIEUX CARRÉS

LES CASSEROLES

MUFFINS ET PLUS

LES DÎNERS

LES BARBECUES (May, 1992)

LES TARTES (September, 1992)

DÉLICES DES FÊTES (October, 1992)

table of Contents

the Jean Paré story

Jean Paré was born and raised during the Great Depression in Irma, a small rural town in eastern Alberta, Canada. She grew up understanding that the combination of family, friends and home cooking is the essence of a good life. Jean learned from her mother, Ruby Elford, to appreciate good cooking and was encouraged by her father, Edward Elford, who praised even her earliest attempts. When she left home she took with her many acquired family recipes, her love of cooking and her intriguing desire to read recipe books like novels!

While raising a family of four, Jean was always busy in her kitchen preparing delicious, tasty treats and savory meals for family and friends of all ages. Her reputation flourished as the mom who would happily feed the neighborhood.

In 1963, when her children had all reached school age, Jean volunteered to cater to the 50th anniversary of the Vermilion School of Agriculture, now Lakeland College. Working out of her home, Jean prepared a dinner for over 1000 people which launched a flourishing catering operation that continued for over eighteen years. During that time she was provided with countless opportunities to test new ideas with immediate feedback – resulting in empty plates and contented customers! Whether preparing cocktail sandwiches for a house party or serving a hot meal for 1500 people, Jean Paré earned a reputation for good food, courteous service and reasonable prices.

"Why don't you write a cookbook?" Time and again, as requests for her recipes mounted, Jean was asked that question. Jean's response was to team up with her son Grant Lovig in the fall of 1980 to form Company's Coming Publishing Limited. April 14, 1981 marked the debut of "150 DELICIOUS SQUARES", the first Company's Coming cookbook in what soon would become Canada's most popular cookbook series. Jean released a new title each year for the first six years. The pace quickened and by 1987 the company had begun publishing two titles each year.

Jean Paré's operation has grown from the early days of working out of a spare bedroom in her home to operating a large and fully equipped test kitchen in Vermilion, Alberta, near the home she and her husband Larry built. Full time staff has grown steadily to include marketing personnel located in major cities across Canada plus selected U.S. markets. Home Office is located in Edmonton, Alberta where distribution, accounting and administration functions are headquartered in the company's own recently constructed 20,000 square foot facility. Company's Coming cookbooks are now distributed throughout Canada and the United States plus numerous overseas markets. Translation of the series to the Spanish and French languages began in 1990.

Jean Paré's approach to cooking has always called for easy-to-follow recipes using mostly common, affordable ingredients. Her wonderful collection of time-honored recipes, many of which are family heirlooms, is a welcome addition to any kitchen. That's why we say: taste the tradition.

Call me sometime ... we'll have lunch!

Foreword

Lunch is the most versatile of meals. You can count on it for everything from a midday spread to a moonlight snack. Creating the perfect menu for a wide variety of situations can be a challenge.

Lunches presents a host of suggestions to make your table sparkle. Versatile and fun, you can follow menus that cater especially to ladies, the young crowd, unexpected visitors on a Sunday afternoon, or last minute invited guests after a game.

This book is divided into sections so you can easily find suitable menus and recipes. Menus are listed at the beginning of each section. For instance, if you're preparing a ladies' luncheon, turn to Especially Ladies'. You may choose to serve the Cheese Soufflé or Cool Raspberry. If you need to satisfy bigger appetites, perhaps some soup from Salads, Sandwiches and Soups followed by Lazy Chicken Enchiladas from Full Lunches will hit the spot. Hamburgers and Chips from Young Crowd Appeal are always a hit with the kids.

For pleasant day-to-day choices, check out From The Shelf. When it's time for a quick, light lunch, Creamed Asparagus On Toast is great. Some of the sandwiches make really pleasing visual presentations. And don't overlook the fruit or shrimp salads; they are perfect meals in themselves. Just serve with a side plate of toast.

Sloppy Joes and Coleslaw from Just In Case are perfect solutions when you're not sure how many hungry people are expected, when they'll arrive, or how famished they'll be. Most recipes from this section, and others throughout the book, can be frozen. Although most cooked foods can be frozen, for best presentation and results, dishes should be prepared and served fresh and leftovers frozen.

Many of the menus are complete with the addition of fresh dinner rolls or pickles purchased from your favorite grocery store. It's a good idea to have some on hand. Most recipes serve four people, so if you know a dish is especially popular, consider doubling it.

This collection of lunch recipes is everything from light and fun to full and splendid. The index is cross-referenced so that you may make additional selections of recipes to change or enhance the suggested menus. Whether you gather on your patio on a warm summer evening or around a big table on a cozy winter afternoon, it's lunch time!

Jean Paré

MENU ONE

Shrimp Newburg   page 9
Tossed Salad   page 14
Dinner Rolls
Pickles
Lemon Filled Cake   page 21
Coffee   Tea

MENU TWO

Chicken In The Shell   page 12
Confetti Cole Slaw   page 13
Hot Buttered Rolls
Pickles
Chilled Dessert   page 20
Coffee   Tea

MENU THREE

Cool Raspberry   page 11
Green Goddess Salad   page 15
Spiced Peaches   page 20
Yeast Pastry Ring   page 26
Curaçao Cheesecake   page 24
Coffee   Tea

MENU FOUR

Cheese Soufflé   page 15
Iceberg Salad   page 11
Sour Cream Biscuits   page 13
Olives, Gherkins
Instant Pistachio Squares   page 16
Coffee   Tea

MENU FIVE

Fruit Salad   page 22
Buttered Toast
Apple Roll Up   page 25
Ice Cream
Coffee   Tea

MENU SIX

Chicken Divan   page 10
Rice Casserole   page 19
Smooth Colleen   page 9
Spiced Apricots   page 19
Cranberry Sauce
Vanilla Muffins   page 14
Lemon Cheese Squares   page 23
Coffee   Tea

SHRIMP NEWBURG

Shrimp in a creamy sauce. Tasty.

Butter or margarine	1/3 cup	75 mL
All-purpose flour	1/3 cup	75 mL
Salt	1/2 tsp.	2 mL
Pepper	1/8 tsp.	0.5 mL
Milk	1 cup	225 mL
Cream	1/2 cup	125 mL
Ketchup	3 tbsp.	50 mL
Lemon juice	1 tsp.	5 mL
Worcestershire sauce	1 1/2 tsp.	7 mL
Cooked shrimp	1 lb.	454 g
Sherry (or alcohol-free sherry)	2 tbsp.	30 mL

Melt butter in large saucepan. Mix in flour, salt and pepper. Add milk and cream, stirring until it boils and thickens.

Stir in ketchup, lemon juice and Worcestershire sauce.

Add shrimp and sherry. Heat slowly stirring often. Freeze leftovers. Serves 4.

SMOOTH COLLEEN

A refreshing, mild, molded salad.

Lime flavored gelatin	3 oz.	85 g
Pineapple juice	1 cup	250 mL
Cottage cheese, smoothed in blender	1 cup	250 mL
Whipping cream (or 1/2 envelope topping)	1/2 cup	125 mL
Frilly lettuce leaves (optional)	4-8	4-8

Combine gelatin and pineapple juice in small saucepan over medium heat. Stir to dissolve. Chill until syrupy.

Stir smoothed cottage cheese into gelatin mixture.

Beat cream until stiff. Fold into gelatin. Turn into individual molds or into 3 cup (750 mL) mold.

Unmold onto lettuce leaves. Garnish with lime slice. Serves 4 to 6.

Pictured on page 17.

CHICKEN DIVAN

This is ideal for a special time. Can be made one day and served the next. Just finish in the oven.

Large chicken breasts, skin removed, halved, boned	4 lbs.	1.8 kg
Celery rib, cut up	1	1
Carrot, cut up	1	1
Salt	2 tsp.	10 mL
Water to cover		
Broccoli, use florets only	2 lbs.	900 g
Boiling salted water		
Condensed cream of chicken soup	10 oz.	284 mL
Salad dressing (or mayonnaise)	1/2 cup	125 mL
Reserved chicken broth	1/2 cup	125 mL
Curry powder	1 tsp.	5 mL
Grated medium Cheddar cheese	1 cup	250 mL
Dry bread crumbs, sprinkle		

Place chicken, celery, carrot and salt in large saucepan. Add water to cover. Cook until tender about 35 minutes. Remove bones. Cut meat in large slices or pieces. Arrange chicken in center of 9 × 13 inch (22 × 33 cm) pan. Measure and reserve 1/2 cup (125 mL) broth.

Cook broccoli in boiling salted water just until tender. Drain. Arrange around chicken.

Mix soup, salad dressing, reserved chicken broth and curry powder. Pour over casserole.

Sprinkle with cheese and bread crumbs. Bake uncovered in 350°F (180°C) oven until hot and cheese is melted about 35 minutes. Leftovers can be frozen. Serves 6.

They wanted protection from theft in their hat factory so they bought a cap gun.

COOL RASPBERRY

So good that you can pretend you are eating dessert first.

Cooking apples, peeled and sliced (McIntosh is good)	3	3
Water	1 cup	250 mL
Raspberry flavored gelatin	3 oz.	85 g
Frozen raspberries in heavy syrup, partially thawed	10 oz.	284 g
SECOND LAYER		
Whipping cream (or 1 envelope topping)	1 cup	250 mL
Cream cheese, softened	4 oz.	125 g
Granulated sugar	2 tbsp.	30 mL
Vanilla	1 tsp.	5 mL

Cook apples in water until soft.

Add gelatin and stir to dissolve.

Add raspberries with syrup. Stir until completely thawed. Pour into 8 x 8 inch (20 x 20 cm) pan. Chill until firm.

Second Layer: Beat cream until stiff. Set aside.

Using same beaters beat cheese, sugar and vanilla together until smooth and light. Fold into whipped cream. Spread over gelatin. Chill. Cuts into 9 squares.

ICEBERG SALAD

A head of iceberg lettuce sets the pace for this salad.

Iceberg lettuce, small head, cut up	1	1
Cherry tomatoes, whole or halved	12	12
Medium-small cucumber, sliced	1	1
Creamy Italian dressing	1/4 cup	50 mL

Combine lettuce, tomatoes and cucumber in large bowl. Chill.

Just before serving add dressing and toss well. Serves 4.

CHICKEN IN THE SHELL

Puff pastry shells overflowing with chicken sauce. Good on toast too. May be served as an appetizer or main course.

Patty shells (puff pastry shells)	8	8
FILLING		
Butter or margarine	1/4 cup	60 mL
Grated carrot	1/2 cup	125 mL
All-purpose flour	1/4 cup	60 mL
Chicken bouillon powder	2 tsp.	10 mL
Salt	1 tsp.	5 mL
Pepper	1/8 tsp.	0.5 mL
Onion powder	1/4 tsp.	1 mL
Milk	3 cups	700 mL
Cooked chicken, chopped	2 cups	500 mL
Canned sliced mushrooms, drained	10 oz.	284 mL
Chopped pimiento	2 tbsp.	30 mL

Cook patty shells according to package directions.

Filling: Melt butter in large saucepan. Add carrot. Sauté until soft and cooked. Do not brown.

Sprinkle flour, bouillon powder, salt, pepper and onion powder over carrot. Mix in. Add milk stirring until it boils and thickens.

Add chicken, mushrooms and pimiento. Heat through.

Spoon into and over patty shells. Filling freezes well. Serves 4.

Pictured on page 17.

The accountant should have no trouble getting a job with the circus. He's been juggling books for years.

CONFETTI COLESLAW

Contains red tomatoes and green onions. Different from the usual slaw. Very good.

Grated cabbage, packed	3 cups	750 mL
Medium carrot, grated	1	1
Chopped green onion	2 tbsp.	30 mL
Tomato, chopped	1	1
DRESSING		
Salad dressing (or mayonnaise)	1/2 cup	125 mL
Milk	2 tbsp.	30 mL
Prepared mustard	1/2 tsp.	2 mL
Granulated sugar	1 tsp.	5 mL
Onion powder	1/4 tsp.	1 mL
Celery seed	1/4 tsp.	1 mL
Salt	1/8 tsp.	0.5 mL

Combine first 4 ingredients in bowl. Mix lightly. Chill.

Dressing: Mix all 7 ingredients. Pour over salad. Toss and serve. Makes 4 servings.

SOUR CREAM BISCUITS

Sour cream provides both the liquid and the shortening in these biscuits. Easy to make.

All-purpose flour	2 cups	500 mL
Granulated sugar	1 1/2 tbsp.	25 mL
Baking powder	4 tsp.	20 mL
Baking soda	1/2 tsp.	2 mL
Salt	1 tsp.	5 mL
Sour cream	1 1/2 cups	375 mL

Measure first 5 ingredients into bowl. Stir.

Add sour cream and stir to form soft ball. Pat or roll 3/4 inch (2 cm) thick on lightly floured surface. Arrange on greased baking sheet. Bake in 425°F (220°C) oven for about 12 to 15 minutes until browned. Freezes well. Makes 16.

TOSSED SALAD

A cheery salad with cheese, radish and green onion.

Head lettuce, cut or torn, lightly packed	4 cups	1 L
Grated medium Cheddar cheese	½ cup	125 mL
Fresh or frozen peas, cooked and cooled	1 cup	250 mL
Radishes, thinly sliced	4-6	4-6
Green onions, sliced	2	2
Salad dressing (or mayonnaise)	⅓ cup	75 mL
Milk	2 tbsp.	30 mL
Granulated sugar	½ tsp.	2 mL

Combine first 5 ingredients in large bowl. Chill.

Mix salad dressing, milk and sugar in small bowl. Just before serving drizzle or pour over salad. Toss to coat. Serves 4.

Pictured on page 17.

VANILLA MUFFINS

These muffins go with everything.

Butter or margarine, softened	¼ cup	60 mL
Granulated sugar	⅓ cup	75 mL
Eggs	2	2
Vanilla	1 tsp.	5 mL
Milk	⅔ cup	150 mL
All-purpose flour	2 cups	450 mL
Baking powder	4 tsp.	20 mL
Salt	1 tsp.	5 mL

Cream butter and sugar together. Beat in eggs. Add vanilla and milk. Mix.

Add flour, baking powder and salt. Stir just until moistened. Fill greased muffin cups ¾ full. Bake in 400°F (200°C) oven for about 20 to 25 minutes until an inserted toothpick comes out clean. Freezes well. Makes 12.

GREEN GODDESS SALAD

Dressing contains chopped parsley and anchovy paste.

GREEN GODDESS DRESSING

Salad dressing (or mayonnaise)	¹/₃ cup	75 mL
Sour cream	¹/₃ cup	75 mL
Chopped green onion	1¹/₂ tbsp.	25 mL
Chopped parsley (or ¹/₂ tsp., 2 mL, flakes)	1¹/₂ tbsp.	25 mL
Anchovy paste	2 tsp.	10 mL
Lemon juice	1¹/₂ tsp.	7 mL
Tarragon flakes	¹/₂ tsp.	2 mL
Head lettuce, cut bite size, lightly packed	10 cups	2.5 L

Green Goddess Dressing: Combine first 7 ingredients in bowl. Mix well. Chill a few hours or overnight if possible. Makes 1 cup (250 mL).

Cut lettuce into large bowl. Pour about ¹/₂ dressing over top and toss. Add more dressing as desired and toss again. Serves 8.

CHEESE SOUFFLÉ

If you have never made a soufflé this is the one to try. Great texture and flavor. Fantastic!

Milk	1¹/₃ cups	300 mL
Minute tapioca	¹/₄ cup	60 mL
Salt	1 tsp.	5 mL
Grated medium Cheddar cheese	1 cup	250 mL
Egg whites, room temperature	4	4
Egg yolks	4	4

Measure milk, tapioca and salt into saucepan. Heat and stir over medium heat until it boils. Remove from heat.

Add cheese. Stir until melted and blended.

Beat egg whites until they hold stiff peaks. Set aside.

Beat egg yolks in small bowl until thick and lemon colored. Stir tapioca mixture into egg yolks. Stir briskly to avoid lumping. Fold this mixture into egg whites. Turn into straight-sided, ungreased 6 cup (1.35 mL) soufflé or baking dish. With a knife cut a line 1 inch (2.5 cm) from edge all around top. Set in pan containing some hot water. Bake in 350°F (180°C) oven until center of top is firm, about 40 minutes. Serve immediately. Freezing not recommended. Serves 4 to 6.

INSTANT PISTACHIO SQUARES

Very light and very good. Can be made ahead and stored in the refrigerator.

CRUST

Butter or margarine	¹/₃ cup	75 mL
Graham cracker crumbs	1¹/₂ cups	350 mL
Granulated sugar	3 tbsp.	50 mL

FILLING

Crushed pineapple with juice	14 oz.	398 mL
Pistachio instant pudding, 4 serving size	1	1
Tiny white marshmallows	2 cups	500 mL
Whipping cream (or 1 envelope topping)	1 cup	250 mL

Crust: Melt butter in small saucepan. Stir in graham crumbs and sugar. Measure and reserve ¹/₄ cup (50 mL) for topping. Pack remaining crumbs into ungreased 9 × 9 inch (22 × 22 cm) pan.

Filling: In medium size bowl stir pineapple with juice and pudding powder together. Add marshmallows. Stir. Let stand 1 hour.

Beat cream until stiff. Fold into pudding mixture. Spread over crumb base. Sprinkle with reserved crumbs. Chill. Cuts into 9 pieces.

RICE CASSEROLE

The topping of Jack cheese and almonds turns this into a company dish.

Water	3 cups	750 mL
Long grain rice	1½ cups	375 mL
Salt	¾ tsp.	4 mL
Butter or margarine	1½ tbsp.	25 mL
Finely chopped onion	⅓ cup	75 mL
Grated Monterey Jack cheese	1½ cups	375 mL
Parsley flakes	1½ tsp.	7 mL
Sour cream	1½ cups	375 mL
Grated Monterey Jack cheese	1½ cups	375 mL
Sliced or slivered almonds	3 tbsp.	50 mL

Combine water, rice and salt in saucepan. Bring to a boil. Simmer covered about 15 minutes until rice is cooked and water is absorbed.

Melt butter in small frying pan. Add onion. Sauté until soft. Add to rice.

Add first amount of cheese, parsley flakes and sour cream to rice. Turn into 2½ quart (3 L) casserole.

Sprinkle with remaining cheese and almonds. Bake uncovered in 350°F (180°C) oven about 30 minutes until heated through and browned. Freeze leftovers. Serves 6.

SPICED APRICOTS

A colorful accompaniment.

Canned apricots, drained, reserve syrup	14 oz.	398 mL
Reserved syrup		
Brown sugar	3 tbsp.	50 mL
Vinegar	1 tbsp.	15 mL
Cinnamon	⅛ tsp.	0.5 mL
Nutmeg	⅛ tsp.	0.5 mL
Ginger	⅛ tsp.	0.5 mL

Halve apricots. Discard pits.

Pour reserved syrup into small saucepan. Add remaining ingredients. Bring to a boil. Simmer slowly as you add apricot halves. Simmer for 10 minutes. Cool. Remove apricots with a slotted spoon. Place in small serving dish. Serves 4.

Pictured on page 53.

CHILLED DESSERT

A mild chocolate nutty filling on a wafer crust.

CRUST

Vanilla wafer crumbs	1¼ cups	275 mL
Butter or margarine, softened	¼ cup	60 mL

FILLING

Whipping cream (or 1 envelope topping)	1 cup	250 mL
Butter or margarine, softened	½ cup	125 mL
Milk	¼ cup	60 mL
Vanilla	1 tsp.	5 mL
Icing (confectioner's) sugar	2 cups	500 mL
Cocoa	3 tbsp.	50 mL
Chopped pecans or walnuts	¾ cup	175 mL

Crust: Mix wafer crumbs and butter until crumbly. Press about half of crumbs in ungreased 8 × 8 inch (20 × 20 cm) pan.

Filling: Beat cream in small mixing bowl until stiff. Set aside.

Combine butter, milk, vanilla, icing sugar and cocoa in separate bowl. Using same beaters beat very slowly at first so milk won't spatter. Now beat until light and fluffy.

Stir in nuts. Fold in cream. Spread over crumb crust in pan. Sprinkle with remaining crumbs. Chill for several hours or overnight. Cuts into 9 pieces.

SPICED PEACHES

Adds a bright spot to any plate.

Boiling water	⅓ cup	75 mL
Minute rice	⅓ cup	75 mL
Salt, just a pinch		
Brown sugar	1 tbsp.	15 mL
Cinnamon	⅛ tsp.	0.5 mL
Butter or margarine	1 tsp.	5 mL
Canned peach halves, drained	4	4
Sliced or slivered almonds	20-30	20-30

(continued on next page)

Combine boiling water, rice and salt in small saucepan. Let steam over low heat until tender. Remove from heat.

Add sugar, cinnamon and butter. Mix well.

Arrange peach halves cut side up in small baking pan or on broiler tray. Fill centers with rice mixture.

Poke almonds into rice mixture. Broil for 4 to 5 minutes. Place beside, but not touching, salads. Serves 4. Double recipe to serve 8.

LEMON FILLED CAKE

A lovely lemon layered loaf cake with very thin layers of cake. A light and refreshing end to a lunch.

Lemon pudding and pie filling (1 pie size)	1	1
Egg yolks	2	2
Egg whites, room temperature	2	2
Ready made pound cake, part or all	12 oz.	341 g
Whipping cream (or 1 envelope topping)	1 cup	250 mL
Granulated sugar	2 tsp.	10 mL
Vanilla	1/2 tsp.	2 mL

Prepare lemon pie filling using 2 egg yolks as package directs. Remove from heat.

Beat egg whites in small mixing bowl until stiff. Fold into hot filling.

Cut cake into 1/3 to 1/2 inch (8 to 12 mm) thick slices. Line 9 x 5 inch (23 x 12 cm) loaf pan with foil. Layer as follows, then chill.

1. Cake slices
2. 1/2 lemon filling
3. Cake slices
4. 1/2 lemon filling
5. Cake slices

Beat cream, sugar and vanilla until thick, in small bowl. Either serve pieces topped with whipped cream or cover top and sides of each piece, or frost whole loaf before cutting. Serves 4 with lots leftover.

FRUIT SALAD

A versatile salad. Adjust quantities to compensate your choice of fruits. A great lunch. A meal in itself.

DRESSING

Cooking oil	1 tbsp.	15 mL
Honey	1/4 cup	60 mL
Vinegar	4 tsp.	20 mL
Celery seed	1/2 tsp.	2 mL
Paprika	1/4 tsp.	1 mL
Salt	1/4 tsp.	1 mL
Pepper	1/16 tsp.	0.5 mL

SALAD

Cottage cheese	2 cups	500 mL
Pink grapefruit, peeled and cut bite size	1	1
Orange, peeled and cut bite size	1	1
Watermelon, peeled and cut bite size	1 cup	250 mL
Cantaloupe cut in balls or pieces or raspberries	1 cup	250 mL
Kiwifruit, peeled and cut bite size	2	2
Sliced strawberries	1 cup	250 mL
Banana, peeled and sliced	1	1
Bread slices, toasted and buttered	8-10	8-10

Dressing: Mix all 7 ingredients well.

Salad: Place a scoop of cottage cheese in center of 4 plates.

Arrange next 7 fruits in groups around cottage cheese. Drizzle with dressing just before serving. If you prefer, fruit may be all tossed together with dressing and then spooned around cottage cheese.

Serve with toast cut in diagonal pieces. Serves 4.

Pictured on page 89.

A light dessert. Not too sweet.

CRUST		
Butter or margarine	1/3 cup	75 mL
Graham cracker crumbs	1 1/4 cups	275 mL
Granulated sugar	2 tbsp.	30 mL
FILLING		
Lemon flavored gelatin	3 oz.	85 g
Boiling water	1 cup	225 mL
Cream cheese, softened	8 oz.	250 g
Granulated sugar	1/2 cup	125 mL
Lemon juice	2 tbsp.	30 mL
Whipping cream (or 1 envelope topping)	1 cup	250 mL
Reserved crumbs	3 tbsp.	50 mL

Crust: Melt butter in saucepan. Stir in graham crumbs and sugar. Measure and reserve 3 tbsp. (50 mL) crumbs for topping. Press remaining crumbs into ungreased 9 × 9 inch (22 × 22 cm) pan. Set aside.

Filling: Dissolve gelatin in boiling water in bowl.

In small mixing bowl beat cream cheese, sugar and lemon juice together until smooth. Slowly beat in warm gelatin. Chill until it starts to set.

Beat cream until stiff. Fold into mixture. Pour over crust in pan.

Sprinkle with reserved crumbs. Chill. Cuts into 9 to 12 pieces.

His sermon was well timed. The congregation kept looking at their watches.

CURAÇAO CHEESECAKE

This KER-a-sow cheesecake is very delicate. Flavor is excellent.

CRUST

Butter or margarine	1/3 cup	75 mL
Graham cracker crumbs	1 1/4 cups	275 mL
Brown sugar	2 tbsp.	30 mL

FILLING

Unflavored gelatin	2 x 1/4 oz.	2 x 7 g
Water	1/3 cup	75 mL
Cream cheese, softened	8 oz.	250 g
Cottage cheese	1 cup	250 mL
Sour cream	1/2 cup	125 mL
Granulated sugar	1/2 cup	125 mL
Grated rind of orange	1	1
Juice of orange	1	1
Orange Curaçao liqueur	3 tbsp.	50 mL
Whipping cream (or 1 envelope topping)	1 cup	250 mL

TOPPING

Whipping cream (or 1/2 envelope topping)	1/2 cup	125 mL
Granulated sugar	1 tsp.	5 mL
Vanilla	1/2 tsp.	2 mL

Mandarin orange segments (optional)

Crust: Melt butter in saucepan. Stir in graham crumbs and sugar. Press into ungreased 8 inch (20 cm) springform pan. Chill.

Filling: Sprinkle gelatin over water in small saucepan. Let stand 5 minutes. Heat and stir to dissolve.

In mixing bowl beat cream cheese and cottage cheese together until smooth. Beat in next 5 ingredients in order given. Add gelatin mixture and beat.

Beat cream until stiff. Fold into cheese mixture. Turn into prepared pan. Chill. Remove pan sides.

Topping: Beat cream, sugar and vanilla together until stiff. Pipe around edge of cake.

Place orange segments on cream on top of each piece or directly on cake. Serves 8 to 12.

Pictured on page 71.

This dessert is so attractive and appetizing. It's hard to believe that it actually tastes as good as it looks.

All-purpose flour	2 cups	450 mL
Baking powder	1 tsp.	5 mL
Salt	1/2 tsp.	2 mL
Butter or margarine	6 tbsp.	100 mL
Milk	3/4 cup	175 mL
Cooking apples, peeled, cored and chopped (McIntosh is good)	4 cups	1 L
Water	2 cups	450 mL
Granulated sugar	1 1/2 cups	375 mL

Butter or margarine, to dot
Granulated sugar, sprinkle
Cinnamon, sprinkle

Vanilla ice cream

Measure first 4 ingredients into bowl. Cut in butter until crumbly.

Add milk. Mix to form ball of dough. Roll out 1/4 inch (6 mm) thick in rectangle about 9 x 12 inch (22 x 30 cm) size.

Spread apple over dough. Roll up from short end.

Boil water and first amount of sugar in small saucepan slowly for 5 minutes. Pour into 9 x 13 inch (22 x 33 cm) pan.

Cut roll into 1 1/2 inch (4 cm) thick slices. Lay slices cut side down in syrup in pan.

Dot with butter. Combine sugar and cinnamon and sprinkle over top. Bake in 450°F (230°C) oven for about 25 minutes until apples are tender.

Serve hot with ice cream. Leftovers can be frozen. Makes about 6.

Yes, he's a lingerie salesman. He keeps giving her the slip.

YEAST PASTRY RING

Spectacular!

Loaf of frozen white bread dough, thawed	1	1
Glazed cut mixed fruit	³/₄ cup	175 mL
Cinnamon	½ tsp.	2 mL
Brown sugar	2 tbsp.	30 mL
ICING		
Icing (confectioner's) sugar	½ cup	125 mL
Lemon juice	1 tbsp.	15 mL
Glazed cherries, quartered	6	6
Sliced almonds, toasted in 350°F (180°C) oven 5 to 10 minutes	2 tbsp.	30 mL

Roll out dough on lightly floured surface to 10 × 14 inch (25 × 35 cm) rectangle.

Sprinkle fruit over dough.

Mix cinnamon and brown sugar. Sprinkle over fruit. Dampen 1 long and 2 short sides of dough with water. Roll from long dry edge to form a roll. Seal at seam. Place in greased 12 cup (2.7 L) bundt pan. Seal ends together. Cover and let stand in warm area until doubled in bulk. Bake in 400°F (200°C) oven about 30 minutes until browned . Cool and ice.

Icing: Mix icing sugar and lemon juice in small pitcher. Add more of either ingredient as required, to make a barely pourable glaze. Spoon over top allowing some to run down sides.

Gently push cherries and almonds in icing around top area. Freezes well. Serves 8.

Pictured on page 17.

Did you hear about the sardine factory that canned all its employees?

FROM THE SHELF

MENU ONE

Corned Beef Shortcake   page 38
Glazed Carrots   page 28
Orange Salad   page 32
Baked Custard   page 28
Coffee   Tea

MENU TWO

Potato Cream Soup   page 34
Crackers
Creamed Chicken on Toast   page 33
Brandied Pear Dessert   page 31
Coffee   Tea

MENU THREE

Luncheon Fry   page 29
Buttered Noodles   page 133
Mixed Beans   page 32
Pickles
Corn Biscuits   page 28
Gingerbread Dessert   page 37
Lemon Sauce   page 128
Coffee   Tea

MENU FOUR

Glazed Ham   page 33
Quick Rice   page 30
Creamed Corn   page 31
Pickles
Dinner Rolls
Dumplings In Syrup   page 39
Coffee   Tea

MENU FIVE

Crab Bisque   page 30
Creamed Asparagus On Toast   page 29
Peach Cobbler   page 38
Coffee   Tea

BAKED CUSTARD

A light, wholesome dessert.

Eggs	3	3
Milk	2 cups	450 mL
Granulated sugar	1/4 cup	50 mL
Vanilla	1 tsp.	5 mL
Salt	1/4 tsp.	1 mL

Nutmeg, sprinkle

Beat eggs in bowl until frothy. Mix in milk, sugar, vanilla and salt. Pour into 1 quart (1 L) casserole.

Sprinkle with nutmeg. Place casserole in pan of hot water. Bake in 325°F (160°C) oven for about 1 hour. An inserted knife should come out clean. Serves 4.

GLAZED CARROTS

Quick, easy, and colorful. Frozen carrots may be used.

Baby carrots, whole	1 lb.	454 g
Boiling salted water		
Butter or margarine	1 1/2 tbsp.	25 mL
Granulated sugar	1 tsp.	5 mL

Cook carrots in boiling salted water until tender. Drain.

Add butter and sugar. Shake saucepan to glaze carrots. Serves 4.

Pictured on page 53.

CORN BISCUITS

A tender drop biscuit. Cream style corn is the liquid used.

Tea biscuit mix	1 1/2 cups	375 mL
Canned cream style corn	1 cup	250 mL
Butter or margarine, melted	1/2 cup	125 mL

Stir biscuit mix and corn together in bowl.

Drop teaspoonfuls into melted butter. Turn to coat. Arrange on baking sheet. Bake in 400°F (200°C) oven about 15 to 20 minutes until risen and browned. Freezes well. Makes about 12.

CREAMED ASPARAGUS ON TOAST

This is a real treat in spring or any time of year. Can be made from canned or frozen asparagus as well as fresh.

CREAM SAUCE		
Butter or margarine	1/3 cup	75 mL
All-purpose flour	1/3 cup	75 mL
Salt	3/4 tsp.	4 mL
Pepper	1/8 tsp.	0.5 mL
Milk	1 1/2 cups	350 mL
Bread slices, toasted and buttered	8	8
Cooked asparagus spears, fresh, canned or frozen, drained	40	40

Cream Sauce: Melt butter in saucepan. Mix in flour, salt and pepper. Stir in milk until it boils and thickens. Add a bit more milk if sauce is too thick.

Lay 2 slices of toast on each plate. Arrange 5 hot asparagus spears on each slice and spoon cream sauce over top. Serves 4.

LUNCHEON FRY

This is top notch shelf food.

Luncheon meat (such as Prem, Spam, Klik, Kam)	2 × 12 oz.	2 × 341 g
Brown sugar, packed	1 cup	250 mL
Prepared mustard	1 1/2 tsp.	7 mL
Prepared orange juice	6 tbsp.	100 mL

Slice meat about 1/3 inch (8 mm) thick and arrange in frying pan. This may have to be done in 2 batches.

Mix sugar, mustard and orange juice in small bowl. Add a bit more mustard to taste if you like. Pour over meat, spreading on every slice. Turn, browning and glazing both sides. Leftovers may be frozen. Serves 4 generously. One can of luncheon meat may be used. However, servings will be considerably smaller. For 1 can use 1/2 sauce.

CRAB BISQUE

A grand soup rich enough to serve small helpings.

Condensed cream of chicken soup	10 oz.	284 mL
Condensed cream of mushroom soup	10 oz.	284 mL
Milk	1⅓ cups	300 mL
Canned crab, cartilage removed	5 oz.	142 g
Salt	¼ tsp.	1 mL
Pepper	⅛ tsp.	0.5 mL
Sherry (or alcohol-free sherry)	1 tbsp.	15 mL

Combine first 3 ingredients in saucepan over medium-low heat. Stir until smooth.

Add crab, salt, pepper and sherry. Bring to a boil and serve. Freezes well. Makes 4 servings 1 cup (250 mL) each.

QUICK RICE

This instant rice is simmered briefly to make it moist and more tender.

Water	1½ cups	350 mL
Chicken bouillon powder	2 tsp.	10 mL
Butter or margarine	1 tbsp.	15 mL
Salt	½ tsp.	2 mL
Minute rice	1½ cups	350 mL

Measure water, bouillon powder, butter and salt into saucepan over medium heat. Bring to a boil.

Add rice. Stir and cover. Allow to simmer for 1 minute. Add a small amount of boiling water to compensate for the simmering. Stir to check on dryness. Add a bit more boiling water if needed. Freeze leftover rice if desired. Serves 4.

Would you consider hanging a suspended sentence?

BRANDIED PEAR DESSERT

A splendid dessert.

Pears, peeled and sliced	3	3
Raisins	2 tbsp.	30 mL
Chopped walnuts	2 tbsp.	30 mL
Semisweet chocolate chips	2 tbsp.	30 mL
Light corn syrup	2 tbsp.	30 mL
Brandy flavoring	1 tsp.	5 mL
All-purpose flour	2/3 cup	150 mL
Brown sugar, packed	1/3 cup	75 mL
Butter or margarine	1/4 cup	60 mL
Salt	1/8 tsp.	0.5 mL

Arrange pears in 1 quart (1 L) casserole. Scatter raisins, walnuts and chocolate chips over pears.

Mix corn syrup and brandy flavoring. Drizzle over fruit.

Mix flour, sugar, butter and salt in small bowl until crumbly. Sprinkle over fruit. Bake uncovered in 350°F (180°C) oven about 30 to 40 minutes until browned and pears are tender. Serve warm to 4 people.

CREAMED CORN

A tasty cream sauce envelopes these kernels.

Butter or margarine	2 tbsp.	30 mL
All-purpose flour	2 tbsp.	30 mL
Onion powder	1/8 tsp.	0.5 mL
Salt	1/2 tsp.	2 mL
Pepper	1/8 tsp.	0.5 mL
Chopped chives	1 tsp.	5 mL
Milk	1 cup	225 mL
Canned kernel corn, drained	12 oz.	341 mL

Melt butter in saucepan. Mix in flour, onion powder, salt, pepper and chives. Stir in milk until it boils and thickens.

Add corn. Heat through. Add more salt and pepper if desired. You may want to double recipe. Makes 4 small servings.

MIXED BEANS

So quick to add life to these beans.

Canned cut green string beans	14 oz.	398 mL
Canned cut yellow wax beans	14 oz.	398 mL
Butter or margarine	2 tbsp.	30 mL
Salt, sprinkle		
Pepper, sprinkle		
Soy sauce, sprinkle (optional but good)		

Bring beans to a boil in saucepan. Drain. Return to heat to dry existing moisture for a few moments.

Add remaining ingredients and toss or shake. Serves 4 generously.

Pictured on page 53.

ORANGE SALAD

A make ahead salad. Enjoy the next day after flavors have blended.

Canned mandarin oranges, drained well (or use 2 fresh)	10 oz.	284 mL
Very finely chopped green pepper, almost minced	$1/4$ cup	50 mL
Finely minced pimiento	1 tbsp.	15 mL
Chopped green onion	1 tbsp.	15 mL
Chopped parsley	1 tbsp.	15 mL
Salt	$1/8$ tsp.	0.5 mL
Chopped lettuce, lightly packed	3 cups	750 mL
Salad dressing (or mayonnaise)	$1/4$ cup	60 mL
Granulated sugar	$1/2$ tsp.	2 mL

If using canned oranges, simply drain and add to bowl. If using fresh oranges, peel and cut in half lengthwise. Then cut into $1/4$ inch (6 mm) thick slices. Place in bowl.

Add next 5 ingredients. Mix. Chill overnight or at least a few hours.

When ready to serve combine lettuce, salad dressing, and sugar in bowl. Mix well. Cover a large plate or 4 small plates with lettuce. Pile orange salad over top. Serves 4.

Pictured on page 89.

GLAZED HAM

A neat little parcel.

Canned ham	1 1/2 lbs.	681 g
Peach or apricot jam	1/2 cup	125 mL
Cider vinegar	4 tsp.	20 mL
Cloves	1/8 tsp.	0.5 mL

Place whole ham in small roaster. Score top in diamond design.

Mix jam, vinegar and cloves in small bowl. Spoon 3 tbsp. (50 mL) over top of ham. Cover and cook in 350°F (180°C) oven about 20 minutes until sizzling. Remove cover. Continue to baste with remaining sauce until hot and glazed. Place ham on small platter or plate. Spoon any juices and glaze from pan over top. Leftovers may be frozen. Serves 4.

CREAMED CHICKEN ON TOAST

You can make this from your shelf if you have chicken or turkey in the freezer or in cans. Liked by everyone.

Butter or margarine	1 tbsp.	15 mL
Chopped onion	1/2 cup	125 mL
Chopped celery	1/4 cup	60 mL
All-purpose flour	3 tbsp.	50 mL
Condensed cream of mushroom soup	10 oz.	284 mL
Milk	1 3/4 cups	350 mL
Parsley flakes	1/2 tsp.	2 mL
Salt	1/2 tsp.	2 mL
Pepper	1/8 tsp.	0.5 mL
Thyme	1/8 tsp.	0.5 mL
Cooked chicken or turkey, cut up	3 cups	700 mL
Bread slices, toasted and buttered	8	8

Melt butter in heavy saucepan. Add onion and celery. Sauté until soft and clear.

Sprinkle with flour. Mix well. Add next 6 ingredients. Stir until it boils and thickens.

Add chicken and heat through.

Place 2 slices of toast on each plate. Divide creamed chicken among them. Serves 4.

POTATO CREAM SOUP

With staples like potatoes and onions on hand, this soup can be made with ease. Lovely flavor.

Peeled diced potatoes	2½ cups	625 mL
Chopped onion	1½ cups	375 mL
Boiling water		
Condensed cream of mushroom soup	10 oz.	284 mL
Milk	2½ cups	625 mL
Salt	½ tsp.	2 mL
Pepper, generous measure	⅛ tsp.	0.5 mL
Parsley flakes	¼ tsp.	1 mL
Thyme	⅛ tsp.	0.5 mL
Oregano	⅛ tsp.	0.5 mL
Butter or margarine	2 tbsp.	30 mL

Cook potato and onion in boiling water until tender. Drain. Mash together.

Add remaining ingredients. Stir to mix. Heat to simmer for 1 or 2 minutes. Freezes well. Makes 6 cups (1.5L). Serves 4.

1. Crab And Noodles page 96
2. Chicken Zucchini Sandwich page 127
3. Meaty Chili page 84

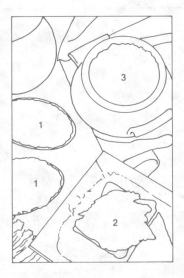

You can whip this up in no time.

Egg	1	1
Cooking oil	1/2 cup	125 mL
Molasses	1/2 cup	125 mL
Granulated sugar	1/2 cup	125 mL
Ginger	3/4 tsp.	4 mL
Cloves	1/4 tsp.	1 mL
Cinnamon	1/4 tsp.	1 mL
Salt	1/2 tsp.	2 mL
Baking soda	1 tsp.	5 mL
Boiling water	1/2 cup	125 mL
All-purpose flour	1 1/2 cups	375 mL
Lemon Sauce, see page 128		
Whipping cream (or 1 envelope topping)	1 cup	250 mL
Granulated sugar	2 tsp.	10 mL
Vanilla	1/2 tsp.	2 mL

Beat egg in mixing bowl until frothy. Beat in cooking oil and molasses. Add first amount of sugar, ginger, cloves, cinnamon and salt. Beat slowly to combine.

Dissolve baking soda in boiling water. Add and mix.

Slowly mix in flour. Turn into greased 8 x 8 inch (20 x 20 cm) pan. Bake in 350°F (180°C) oven about 35 to 40 minutes until an inserted wooden pick comes out clean.

Make Lemon Sauce and keep warm.

Beat cream, second amount of sugar and vanilla in small bowl until stiff. Serve cake warm with Lemon Sauce and whipped cream. Freezes well. Cuts into 9 pieces.

The favorite dessert of sculptors is marble cake of course.

PEACH COBBLER

A good, easy dessert to make from the shelf.

Canned sliced peaches, drained, reserve juice	14 oz.	398 mL
Brown sugar, packed	1/3 cup	75 mL
All-purpose flour	2 tbsp.	30 mL
Salt	1/8 tsp.	0.5 mL
Cinnamon	1/8 tsp.	0.5 mL
Vinegar	1 tbsp.	15 mL
Reserved peach juice		
TOPPING		
All-purpose flour	3/4 cup	175 mL
Granulated sugar	3 tbsp.	50 mL
Baking powder	1 1/2 tsp.	7 mL
Salt	1/4 tsp.	1 mL
Cold butter or margarine	2 1/2 tbsp.	35 mL
Cold milk	6 tbsp.	100 mL

Place sliced peaches in 1 quart (1 L) casserole.

Measure next 4 ingredients into small bowl. Stir to blend.

Add vinegar and reserved peach juice. Stir well and pour over peaches. Place in 425°F (220°C) oven until hot. Meanwhile prepare topping.

Topping: Combine first 5 ingredients in bowl. Cut in butter until crumbly.

Add milk. Stir to moisten. Drop by spoonfuls over hot fruit. Return uncovered to oven about 20 to 25 minutes until risen and browned. Leftovers may be frozen. Serves 4.

CORNED BEEF SHORTCAKE

Another shelf lunch that has a gourmet look when finished.

Butter or margarine	2 tbsp.	30 mL
Chopped onion	1 cup	250 mL
Canned corned beef, broken up	12 oz.	340 g
Condensed cream of mushroom soup	10 oz.	284 mL
Grated medium Cheddar cheese	1 cup	250 mL
Tea biscuit mix	3 cups	700 mL
Cold water	3/4 cup	175 mL

(continued on next page)

Melt first amount of butter in frying pan. Add onion. Sauté until soft. Remove from heat. Cool.

Add corned beef, soup and cheese. Stir well. Keep warm.

Combine biscuit mix and water in bowl. Mix to form a soft ball. Divide into 4 equal balls. Pat each ball 1 inch (2.5 cm) thick. Place 1 biscuit on your hand. Pinch all around to make a bit of an edge. Turn it over and repeat. This causes it to keep its shape when baked. Otherwise it rises into a crooked ball. Make edges top and bottom of other 3 biscuits. Place on ungreased baking sheet. Bake in 425°F (220°C) oven about 15 to 18 minutes until browned. Split biscuits in half. Spoon ³/₄ of corned beef over bottom. Cut cone shaped portions from center of top halves. Place top halves over corned beef mixture forming a sandwich. Spoon remaining corned beef into cut-out centers. Cut cones in half. Turn and place on top to form butterflies. Serves 4.

DUMPLINGS IN SYRUP

Simply yummy.

SYRUP

Brown sugar, packed	¹/₂ cup	125 mL
All-purpose flour	3 tbsp.	50 mL
Water	2 cups	450 mL
Lemon juice	1 tsp.	5 mL
Chopped raisins	2 tbsp.	30 mL
Butter or margarine	1 tbsp.	15 mL
Vanilla	1 tsp.	5 mL
Salt	¹/₄ tsp.	1 mL

DUMPLINGS

All-purpose flour	1 cup	250 mL
Granulated sugar	¹/₂ cup	125 mL
Baking powder	2 tsp.	10 mL
Milk	¹/₂ cup	125 mL
Cooking oil	1 tbsp.	15 mL

Syrup: Combine sugar and flour in saucepan. Mix well. Stir in water and lemon juice. Add raisins, butter, vanilla and salt. Bring to a boil. Simmer about 15 minutes until medium brown in color. Pour into 8 inch (20 cm) casserole.

Dumplings: Measure flour, granulated sugar and baking powder into bowl. Mix well.

Add milk and cooking oil to flour mixture. Mix to soft dough. Drop dough in spoonfuls into syrup in casserole. Bake uncovered in 350°F (180°C) oven about 30 minutes until browned. Serve warm. Makes 4 to 6 generous servings.

FULL LUNCHES

MENU ONE

Shrimp On Rice   page 48
Vegetable Aspic   page 45
Parkerhouse Rolls
Cheesecake Pie   page 62
Coffee   Tea

MENU TWO

Chicken Stew With Dumplings   page 58
Spiced Apple   page 55
Dinner Rolls
Cherry Treat   page 66
Coffee   Tea

MENU THREE

Lazy Chicken Enchiladas   page 44
Avocado Salad   page 50
Cornbread   page 50
Chunky Angel In Chocolate   page 69
Coffee   Tea

MENU FOUR

Ground Beef Roll   page 49
Dilled Potatoes   page 43
Dinner Rolls
Peach Melba   page 68
Coffee   Tea

MENU FIVE

Stew With Pastry   page 46
Coleslaw   page 77
Beet Pickles
Onion Biscuits   page 76
Simple Strawberries   page 62
Coffee   Tea

MENU SIX

Simple Chicken   page 47
Perky Rice   page 69
Cranberry Sauce
Last Minute Biscuits   page 52
Bread Custard Pudding   page 68
Coffee   Tea

MENU SEVEN

Baked Burger   page 60
Mexican Salad   page 45
Dinner Rolls
Pickles
Ice Cream Crisp   page 63
Coffee   Tea

MENU EIGHT

Shepherd's Pie   page 51
Marinated Corn   page 43
Cheese Straws   page 55
Apricot Dessert   page 65
Coffee   Tea

Menu Nine

Pot Roast With Vegetables   page 57
Dinner Rolls
Dill Pickles
Sweet Pickles
Rum Cream Puffs   page 64
Coffee   Tea

Menu Ten

Baked Beans   page 61
Pine-Apple Salad   page 56
Beer Bread   page 61
Pickles
Meringue Pie   page 67
Coffee   Tea

Menu Eleven

Salmon Loaf   page 42
Mushroom Sauce   page 42
Oven Baked Rice   page 44
Tender Biscuits   page 49
Dill Pickles
Raspberry Delight Pie   page 70
Coffee   Tea

Menu Twelve

Beef Rolls   page 59
Chips   page 145
Carrot Salad   page 47
French Bread
Pickles
Cool Chocolate Pie   page 66
Coffee   Tea

Menu Thirteen

Chicken in Gravy   page 60
Buttered Noodles   page 133
Spiced Apricots   page 19
Cucumber Salad Mold   page 56
Tender Biscuits   page 49
Angel's Rainbow Cake   page 73
Coffee   Tea

SALMON LOAF

Use red salmon for the most attractive appearance. Serve with a mushroom sauce.

Canned salmon, drained, skin and round bones removed	2 x 7$\frac{1}{2}$ oz.	2 x 213 g
Dry bread crumbs	$\frac{1}{2}$ cup	125 mL
Parsley flakes	1 tsp.	5 mL
Salt	$\frac{1}{2}$ tsp.	2 mL
Pepper	$\frac{1}{8}$ tsp.	0.5 mL
Lemon juice	1 tbsp.	15 mL
Egg yolks	2	2
Hot milk	$\frac{1}{2}$ cup	125 mL
Butter or margarine	2 tbsp.	30 mL
Egg whites, room temperature	2	2

Place first 7 ingredients into medium size bowl.

Mix hot milk and butter. Add to salmon mixture and stir well.

Beat egg whites in small mixing bowl until stiff. Fold into salmon mixture. Turn into greased 1$\frac{1}{2}$ quart (1.5 L) casserole. Bake in 350°F (180°C) oven for 1 hour. Serve with Mushroom Sauce, below. Freezes well. Serves 4 to 6.

MUSHROOM SAUCE

Butter or margarine	3 tbsp.	50 mL
Sliced fresh mushrooms	1 cup	250 mL
All-purpose flour	2 tbsp.	30 mL
Salt	$\frac{1}{2}$ tsp.	2 mL
Pepper	$\frac{1}{8}$ tsp.	0.5 mL
Paprika	$\frac{1}{2}$ tsp.	2 mL
Chicken bouillon powder	$\frac{1}{2}$ tsp.	2 mL
Milk	1 cup	250 mL
White wine (or alcohol-free wine)	1 tbsp.	15 mL

Melt butter in frying pan. Add mushrooms. Sauté until soft.

Sprinkle with flour, salt, pepper, paprika and bouillon powder. Mix well. Stir in milk and wine until it boils and thickens. Spoon over Salmon Loaf. Makes 1 cup (250 mL).

MARINATED CORN

Add extra color to your plate with this quick pickle.

Granulated sugar	½ cup	125 mL
Salt	¼ tsp.	1 mL
Dry mustard	¼ tsp.	1 mL
Onion powder	¼ tsp.	1 mL
Vinegar	½ cup	125 mL
Cooking oil	1 tbsp.	15 mL
Canned baby corn cobs, drained	14 oz.	398 mL

Stir first 6 ingredients together in bowl until sugar is dissolved.

Add corn. Chill overnight. Serves 4.

DILLED POTATOES

An easy method for a good flavor.

Medium potatoes, peeled and quartered	4	4
Boiling salted water		
Butter or margarine	3 tbsp.	50 mL
Dill weed	½ tsp.	2 mL

Cook potatoes in boiling salted water until tender. Drain.

Add butter and dill weed. Shake pan to melt and coat. Turn into bowl. Serves 4.

Paré Pointer

Everyone is wearing a straw hat. Those hats are having a hay day.

LAZY CHICKEN ENCHILADAS

A non-tomato enchilada casserole. Creamy good.

Chicken parts	2¼ lbs.	1 kg
Water to cover		
Salt	2 tsp.	10 mL
Butter or margarine	2 tbsp.	30 mL
Chopped onion	½ cup	125 mL
All-purpose flour	1 tbsp.	15 mL
Condensed cream of chicken soup	10 oz.	284 mL
Condensed cream of mushroom soup	10 oz.	284 mL
Sour cream	½ cup	125 mL
Canned chopped green chilies	4 oz.	114 mL
Soft flour tortillas, large size	6	6
Grated Monterey Jack cheese	1½ cups	375 mL

Place chicken in water and salt in saucepan. Boil covered, about 30 minutes until tender. Remove skin and bones. Chop meat and set aside.

Melt butter in saucepan. Add onion. Sauté until soft.

Mix in flour. Add next 4 ingredients. Stir until it boils. Add chicken and mix.

Tear tortillas into pieces. Spoon enough chicken mixture into 2 qt. (2.5 L) casserole to cover bottom. Make layer of 3 torn tortillas followed by ½ chicken mixture, 3 more torn tortillas and rest of chicken mixture.

Sprinkle with cheese. Cover. Bake in 350°F (180°C) oven for about 20 minutes. Remove cover and cook for 10 to 15 minutes more. Leftovers may be frozen. Serves 4 generously.

OVEN BAKED RICE

Worry free, light and fluffy.

Long grain rice	1 cup	250 mL
Water	2 cups	500 mL
Butter or margarine	3 tbsp.	50 mL
Parsley flakes	2 tsp.	10 mL
Salt	¼ tsp.	1 mL
Seasoned salt	¼ tsp.	1 mL

Measure all 6 ingredients into 2 quart (2.5 L) casserole. Cover and bake in 350°F (180°C) oven about 45 minutes until tender. Fluff with fork. Leftovers may be frozen. Serves 4.

MEXICAN SALAD

An uncommon salad with an excellent dressing.

Romaine lettuce, torn, lightly packed	4 cups	1 L
Canned chick peas (garbanzo beans), drained	1 cup	250 mL
Avocado, peeled, sliced and cut bite size	1	1

DRESSING		
Granulated sugar	2 tbsp.	30 mL
Vinegar	1½ tbsp.	25 mL
Cooking oil	1 tbsp.	15 mL
Ketchup	1 tbsp.	15 mL
Onion powder	⅛ tsp.	0.5 mL
Worcestershire sauce	¼ tsp.	1 mL

Combine lettuce, chick peas and avocado in large bowl.

Dressing: Mix all 6 ingredients with whisk. Pour over salad and toss. To prepare a short time ahead dip avocado in lemon juice. Chill salad. Add dressing before serving. Serves 4.

Pictured on page 53.

VEGETABLE ASPIC

A sneaky way to serve vegetables.

Unflavored gelatin	1 x ¼ oz.	1 x 7 g
Water	¼ cup	50 mL
Vegetable juice (V8 is good)	1¾ cups	400 mL
Dry onion flakes	1 tsp.	5 mL
Granulated sugar	1 tsp.	5 mL
Salt	⅛ tsp.	0.5 mL
Lemon juice	1 tsp.	5 mL
Peppercorns	2	2
Whole clove	1	1
Finely chopped celery	¼ cup	50 mL
Grated carrot	¼ cup	50 mL
Grated cabbage	¼ cup	50 mL

Sprinkle gelatin over water in small container. Let stand.

Combine next 7 ingredients in saucepan over medium heat. Bring to a boil. Boil slowly for 8 to 10 minutes. Strain liquid into bowl. Stir in gelatin mixture until it dissolves. Chill until syrupy.

Add celery, carrot and cabbage. Chill until set. Serves 4.

STEW WITH PASTRY

Tender cubes of beef cooked with spices and a touch of wine. Crowned with pastry in onion soup bowls. Serve directly from saucepan if you like.

Round steak, cut bite size	1½ lbs.	700 g
Margarine	1 tbsp.	15 mL
Cooking oil	1 tbsp.	15 mL
Sliced onion	1 cup	250 mL
Celery flakes	1 tsp.	5 mL
Salt	1½ tsp.	7 mL
Pepper	¼ tsp.	1 mL
Thyme	⅛ tsp.	0.5 mL
Garlic powder	¼ tsp.	1 mL
Water	2 cups	500 mL
Red wine (or alcohol-free wine)	2 tbsp.	30 mL
Potato cubes	2 cups	500 mL
Carrot cubes (cut smaller than potato)	2 cups	500 mL
Canned whole mushrooms or pieces, drained	10 oz.	284 mL
Pastry, regular or puff		

Add steak a few pieces at a time to margarine and cooking oil in frying pan. As it browns remove to medium size saucepan. Add more margarine and cooking oil to frying pan as needed.

Add next 8 ingredients to saucepan. Stir. Cover and bring to a boil. Simmer until meat is very tender, about 2 hours.

Add potato and carrot to meat adding more water as needed. Cook until tender.

Stir in mushrooms.

Roll pastry 1 inch (2.5 cm) larger in diameter than onion soup bowl. Cut out 4 rounds. Spoon stew into soup bowls. Cover with pastry, pressing edges all around side of bowl. Cut slits in top. Bake in 400°F (200°C) oven about 20 to 25 minutes until browned. Leftover stew can be baked in additional soup bowls or served directly on plates for second helpings. Leftovers may be frozen. Serves 4.

Carrots provide the color and raisins provide the sweetness.

Grated carrot	3 cups	700 mL
Chopped celery	1/2 cup	125 mL
Raisins	1/2 cup	125 mL
Salad dressing (or mayonnaise)	1/2 cup	125 mL
Vinegar	1 tbsp.	15 mL
Granulated sugar	1 1/2 tsp.	7 mL
Prepared mustard	1/4 tsp.	1 mL
Paprika	1/8 tsp.	0.5 mL

Combine carrot, celery and raisins in bowl.

Measure remaining ingredients into another bowl. Mix. Pour over vegetables and toss. Serves 4.

SIMPLE CHICKEN

A snap to make. Just pour sauce over chicken and bake. A teriyaki flavor.

Chicken thighs	8-12	8-12
Soy sauce	1/2 cup	125 mL
Granulated sugar	3 tbsp.	50 mL
Cooking oil	3 tbsp.	50 mL
Salt	1/4 tsp.	1 mL
Pepper	1/8 tsp.	0.5 mL
Ginger	1/4 tsp.	1 mL
Garlic powder	1/4 tsp.	1 mL
Onion powder	1/4 tsp.	1 mL

Arrange chicken skin side down in 9 x 13 inch (22 x 33 cm) pan. Skin may be removed if you like.

Mix remaining 8 ingredients in small bowl. Pour over chicken. Bake uncovered in 375°F (190°C) oven for 45 minutes. Turn chicken pieces skin side up. Bake about 15 minutes more until fork tender. Leftovers can be frozen. Sauce may be thickened by stirring 1 tbsp. (15 mL) each of cornstarch and water, mixed, into 1 cup (225 mL) boiling sauce. Serves 4 people 2 to 3 pieces each.

SHRIMP ON RICE

Breeze through lunch with this goodie in the oven. Excellent.

Water	1½ cups	375 mL
Salt	½ tsp.	2 mL
Minute rice	1½ cups	375 mL
Condensed cream of mushroom soup	10 oz.	284 mL
Milk	⅓ cup	75 mL
Salad dressing (or mayonnaise)	⅓ cup	75 mL
Lemon juice	1 tbsp.	15 mL
Onion powder	¼ tsp.	1 mL
Sherry (or alcohol-free sherry)	2 tbsp.	30 mL
Canned medium or small shrimp, rinsed and drained	4 oz.	113 g
TOPPING		
Butter or margarine	1 tbsp.	15 mL
Dry bread crumbs	¼ cup	50 mL
Grated medium Cheddar cheese	¼ cup	50 mL

Bring water to a boil in medium size saucepan. Add salt and rice. Cover. Remove from heat. Let stand 10 minutes. Turn into ungreased 1½ quart (1.5 L) casserole.

Combine next 6 ingredients in bowl. Stir well.

Carefully fold in shrimp. Pour over rice.

Topping: Melt butter in small saucepan. Stir in bread crumbs and cheese. Sprinkle over casserole. Bake in 350°F (180°C) oven for about 30 minutes until bubbly hot and browned. Leftovers may be frozen. Serves 4.

Paré Pointer

To get the latest headlines, sleep on a corduroy pillow.

TENDER BISCUITS

Very tender and fragile.

Tea biscuit mix	2¼ cups	550 mL
Butter or margarine, softened	¼ cup	60 mL
Water	½ cup	125 mL

Mix all 3 ingredients to make soft ball of dough. Shape into 12 balls and arrange on greased baking sheet leaving room for expansion. Bake in 425°F (220°C) oven for 10 to 15 minutes. Freezes well. Makes 12 to 15.

GROUND BEEF ROLL

Meatloaf in a roll with ham and cheese inside.

Ground beef	1½ lbs.	700 g
Dry bread crumbs	⅓ cup	75 mL
Ketchup	3 tbsp.	50 mL
Egg, beaten	1	1
Parsley flakes	1 tsp.	5 mL
Salt	1 tsp.	5 mL
Pepper	¼ tsp.	1 mL
Oregano	¼ tsp.	1 mL
Garlic powder	¼ tsp.	1 mL
Thin cooked ham slices	6	6
Grated medium Cheddar cheese or mozzarella	1 cup	250 mL
Ketchup for topping		
Cheese slices, cut in half diagonally	3-4	3-4

Combine first 9 ingredients in bowl. Mix well. Pat out on piece of waxed paper making 8 x 12 inch (20 x 30 cm) rectangle.

Cover with ham slices keeping at least ½ inch (12 mm) in from sides. Sprinkle with grated cheese. Roll from short end like a jelly roll, using waxed paper to help lift and roll. Press ends and rolled edge together. Place in greased 9 x 9 inch (22 x 22 cm) pan seam side down. Bake uncovered in 350°F (180°C) oven for 1 hour 20 minutes.

As soon as meat is removed from oven, spread with ketchup and arrange cheese triangles over top. Freezes well. Slice to serve 4.

CORNBREAD

Serve warm wedges for a definite hit.

All-purpose flour	1¼ cups	275 mL
Cornmeal	¾ cup	175 mL
Granulated sugar	2 tbsp.	30 mL
Baking powder	1 tbsp.	15 mL
Salt	1 tsp.	5 mL
Butter or margarine	¼ cup	50 mL
Milk	⅞ cup	200 mL

Measure all ingredients into bowl. Beat with spoon until blended. Turn into greased 8 inch (20 cm) round layer pan. Bake in 400 °F (200°C) oven about 20 to 25 minutes until an inserted toothpick comes out clean. Freezes well. Cuts into 8 to 12 wedges.

Pictured on page 125.

AVOCADO SALAD

You don't have to live in avocado country to enjoy this salad.

DRESSING		
Vinegar	2 tbsp.	30 mL
Granulated sugar	1 tsp.	5 mL
Salt	½ tsp.	2 mL
Pink grapefruit, peeled and sectioned, cut bite size	2	2
Avocado, peeled and sliced, cut bite size	2	2
Green onion, chopped	2	2
Chopped celery	1 cup	250 mL
Crisp lettuce leaves	16	16

Dressing: Mix all 3 ingredients in small bowl.

Place grapefruit in bowl. Add avocado. Mix. Add onion and celery. Pour dressing over fruit. Stir to distribute. Chill.

Lay lettuce 4 leaves thick, on each of 4 plates. Spoon salad over lettuce. Serves 4.

This dish brings back childhood memories.

Cooking oil	1 tbsp.	15 mL
Lean ground beef	1½ lbs.	750 g
Chopped onion	1 cup	250 mL
All-purpose flour	1 tbsp.	15 mL
Salt	1½ tsp.	7 mL
Pepper	¼ tsp.	1 mL
Milk	⅓ cup	75 mL
Ketchup	1 tbsp.	15 mL
Worcestershire sauce	1 tsp.	5 mL
Horseradish	1 tsp.	5 mL
Peas, fresh or frozen, cooked	1 cup	250 mL
Sliced carrots, cooked	1 cup	250 mL
Medium potatoes peeled	4	4
Boiling salted water		
Butter or margarine	1 tbsp.	15 mL
Milk	3-4 tbsp.	45-60 mL
Seasoned salt	½ tsp.	2 mL
Butter or margarine, melted	2 tbsp.	30 mL
Paprika, sprinkle		

Heat cooking oil in frying pan. Add ground beef and onion. Sauté until lightly browned.

Sprinkle with flour, salt and pepper. Mix well. Stir in first amount of milk until it boils.

Add next 5 ingredients. Pack into 8 x 8 inch (20 x 20 cm) pan or casserole.

Cook potatoes in boiling salted water until tender. Drain and mash. Add first amount of butter, second amount of milk and seasoned salt. Mash together. Spread over meat.

Brush with melted butter. Sprinkle with paprika. With fork, make wave pattern in potato. Bake uncovered near top of 350°F (180°C) oven about 30 minutes until hot and lightly browned. Leftovers may be frozen. Serves 4 generously.

LAST MINUTE BISCUITS

Refrigerator biscuits dipped in seasoned melted butter and cheese.

Package of refrigerator biscuits (10 to a carton)	1	1
Butter or margarine	3 tbsp.	50 mL
Parsley flakes	1 tsp.	5 mL
Seasoned salt	1/4 tsp.	1 mL
Grated sharp or medium Cheddar cheese	1/2 cup	125 mL

Separate biscuits.

Melt butter in small saucepan. Stir in parsley and salt. Remove from heat.

Dip biscuit in butter mixture. Shake a bit to allow drops to fall off. Dip in cheese and place in greased 8 inch (20 cm) round layer pan. Sprinkle with remaining cheese. Bake in 400°F (200°C) oven about 20 minutes until risen and well browned. Leftovers may be frozen. Makes 10.

Pictured on page 125.

Crisp and good.

Grated sharp Cheddar cheese	1 cup	250 mL
Butter or margarine, softened	1/2 cup	125 mL
All-purpose flour	1 cup	250 mL
Salt	1/2 tsp.	2 mL
Cayenne pepper	1/8 tsp.	0.5 mL

Cream cheese and butter together until smooth. Mix in flour, salt and cayenne pepper. Dough will be stiff. Roll. Cut in strips about $3/4 \times 2 1/4$ inches (2 x 6 cm). Arrange on ungreased baking sheet. Bake in 325°F (160°C) oven about 15 to 20 minutes. Freezes well. Makes 24.

Pictured on page 125.

Pretty as a picture. Dresses up any plate.

Water	2 cups	500 mL
Granulated sugar	1/2 cup	125 mL
Cinnamon stick, 5 1/2 inches (14 cm) long	1	1
Red food coloring	1/8 tsp.	0.5 mL
Cooking apples, left whole, peeled, cored and sliced in 1/3 inch (8 mm) thick round rings	4	4
Cream cheese, softened	2 oz.	62 g
Grated medium Cheddar cheese	1/4 cup	50 mL
Ground pecans or walnuts	2 tbsp.	30 mL
Small lettuce leaves	4	4

Combine first 4 ingredients in saucepan just large enough so liquid is deeper than apple slices. Cover and bring to a boil. Simmer slowly for 4 minutes. Remove cinnamon stick.

Arrange apple slices in red juice a few at a time. Liquid should cover. Return to a boil. Simmer slowly about 10 minutes until point of sharp knife pierces apple easily. Turn once. Remove gently and cool.

Work cream cheese with a spoon until soft. Add Cheddar cheese. Mix well. Roll into as many balls as you have apple slices.

Roll balls in pecans. Place in center of apple slices.

Place apple slices on lettuce. Serves 4.

PINE-APPLE SALAD

A fruit and cheese mixture in a fluffy dressing. Excellent.

Crushed pineapple, drained	1/2 cup	125 mL
Diced celery	1/3 cup	75 mL
Apples with peel, diced	2	2
Grated medium Cheddar cheese	1/2 cup	125 mL
Finely chopped walnuts	2 tbsp.	30 mL
Whipping cream (or 1/2 envelope topping)	1/2 cup	125 mL
Salad dressing (or mayonnaise)	1/3 cup	75 mL
Granulated sugar	1 tbsp.	15 mL

Combine pineapple, celery, apple, cheese and walnuts in bowl. To prevent apple from browning, toss immediately to mix well.

Beat cream in small bowl until stiff.

Fold salad dressing and sugar into cream. Add to salad. Fold in gently. Serves 4.

CUCUMBER SALAD MOLD

Milky green in color. A refreshing salad.

Lime flavored gelatin	3 oz.	85 g
Dry onion flakes	1 tbsp.	15 mL
Boiling water	3/4 cup	175 mL
Lemon juice	4 tsp.	20 mL
Salt	1/2 tsp.	2 mL
Horseradish	1 tsp.	5 mL
Sour cream	1/3 cup	75 mL
Salad dressing (or mayonnaise)	1/3 cup	75 mL
Grated peeled cucumber, drained well	3/4 cup	175 mL

Pour gelatin and onion flakes into bowl. Add boiling water. Stir to dissolve gelatin.

Add lemon juice, salt and horseradish. Chill until syrupy.

Mix in sour cream, salad dressing and cucumber. Pour into serving dish or 2 1/2 cup (500 mL) or a bit larger mold. Makes 4 medium-small servings.

POT ROAST WITH VEGETABLES

Old fashioned dish to be sure. As good now as ever.

Cooking oil	2 tbsp.	30 mL
Boneless beef pot roast	2½ lbs.	1.23 kg
All-purpose flour		
Salt	1½ tsp.	7 mL
Pepper	¼ tsp.	1 mL
Water	1 cup	250 mL
Medium carrots, scraped and halved	6	6
Medium onions, peeled and quartered	2	2
Medium potatoes, peeled and halved	4	4
Turnip, size of large orange, cut in 8 pieces	1	1
All-purpose flour	3 tbsp.	50 mL
Water	6 tbsp.	100 mL

Heat cooking oil in large heavy saucepan or Dutch oven. Coat meat with flour. Place in saucepan and brown well on all sides.

Add salt, pepper and first amount of water. Unless pan is very heavy, place small rack under meat. Small jam jar lids with holes punched through work well. Cover and cook slowly for about 2 hours. Add more water if necessary.

Add carrots, onions, potatoes and turnip. Continue to cook until vegetables are tender, about 30 minutes.

Remove vegetables and meat to hot platter. Cover to keep warm. Measure liquid in pan. Add water to make 2 cups (500 mL). Bring to a boil. Mix second amounts of flour and water in small bowl, until smooth. Stir into boiling liquid to make gravy. Add more water if gravy is too thick. Add salt and pepper as desired. Serves 4.

Paré Pointer

You will find that when you use a pogo stick it makes you jumpy.

CHICKEN STEW WITH DUMPLINGS

These dumplings are actually biscuits cooked with the stew. A meal in one.

Medium potatoes, peeled and cut bite size	2	2
Medium carrots, peeled and cut bite size (smaller than potatoes)	4	4
Large onion, peeled, cut up	1	1
Boiling salted water		
Peas, fresh or frozen	1½ cups	375 mL
Chicken bouillon cubes	2	2
Boiling water	1½ cups	375 mL
Condensed cream of chicken soup	10 oz.	284 mL
Cooked chicken, cut up	3 cups	750 mL
Thyme	¼ tsp.	1 mL
Tea biscuit mix	2 cups	450 mL
Milk	¾ cup	175 mL

Cook potatoes, carrots and onion in boiling salted water until tender.

Add peas. Cook for about 3 minutes more. Drain.

Dissolve bouillon cubes in boiling water in large bowl.

Add soup to bouillon and stir. Add chicken, thyme and vegetables. Turn into 3 quart (4 L) casserole. Heat in 350°F (180°C) oven about 40 minutes until hot.

Stir biscuit mix and milk together. Drop by spoonfuls over hot stew. Turn oven to 425°F (220°C). Cook for about 15 to 20 minutes more, until risen and browned. Leftovers may be frozen. Serves 4 generously.

Nobody shelves as many ideas as a librarian.

This needs a bit of extra time to roll onion and carrot in the meat.
Looks very fancy on each plate served whole or sliced .

Round steak, ½ inch (12 mm) thick	1½ lbs.	700 g
Prepared mustard		
Chopped onion	½ cup	125 mL
Salt, sprinkle		
Pepper, sprinkle		
Carrot sticks	4	4
Margarine (butter browns too fast)	2 tbsp.	30 mL
All-purpose flour	¼ cup	50 mL
GRAVY		
Butter or margarine	3 tbsp.	50 mL
All-purpose flour	3 tbsp.	50 mL
Salt	½ tsp.	2 mL
Water	1½ cups	375 mL
Gravy browner		

Cut steak into 4 pieces.

Spread with mustard. Sprinkle with onion, salt and pepper. Lay carrot stick on each and roll. Secure with string.

Melt margarine in frying pan. Coat rolls with flour. Brown well on all sides. Transfer to 2 quart (2.5 L) casserole.

Gravy: Add butter to frying pan. Mix in flour and salt. Stir in water until it boils and thickens. Add gravy browner to color a bit darker. Loosen all bits in pan. Pour over meat. Cover and cook in 350°F (180°C) oven for about 1½ hours until meat is very tender. Serve whole or sliced on each plate. Freezes well. Serves 4.

I see babes in the wood. I see baby termites.

BAKED BURGER

A layer of meat covered with a Yorkshire pudding topping. Different, good and economical.

Lean ground beef	1½ lbs.	700 g
Chopped onion	1 cup	250 mL
Salt	1 tsp.	5 mL
Pepper	¼ tsp.	1 mL
Worcestershire sauce	1 tsp.	5 mL
Eggs	2	2
Milk	1 cup	250 mL
All-purpose flour	1 cup	250 mL
Salt	½ tsp.	2 mL

Mix ground beef, onion, salt, pepper and Worcestershire sauce in bowl. Pack into 9 × 9 inch (22 × 22 cm) pan. Bake in 350°F (180°C) oven for 20 minutes.

Beat eggs, milk, flour and salt together until very smooth and light. Pour over meat. Continue to bake about 30 to 40 minutes until set. Leftovers may be frozen. Serves 4.

CHICKEN IN GRAVY

So convenient. Ingredients from the shelf with a touch of sherry poured over chicken, then baked.

Chicken breasts, halved	4	4
Margarine (butter browns too fast)	2 tbsp.	30 mL
Condensed cream of mushroom soup	10 oz.	284 mL
Milk	⅓ cup	75 mL
Sherry (or alcohol-free sherry)	2 tbsp.	30 mL
Onion soup mix (envelope)	1	1

Brown chicken on both sides in margarine in frying pan, adding more margarine if needed. Transfer to 3 quart (4 L) casserole.

Combine next 4 ingredients in bowl. Stir well and pour over chicken. Cover and cook in 350°F (180°C) oven about 1 to 1¼ hours until tender. Freezes well. Serves 4.

Pictured on page 53.

Home baked beans are always a good choice. Dark brown in color when baked. Contains ground beef.

Dry navy beans	1 cup	250 mL
Water	3 cups	750 mL
Ketchup	²/₃ cup	150 mL
Brown sugar, packed	¹/₂ cup	125 mL
Molasses	2 tbsp.	30 mL
Salt	¹/₂ tsp.	2 mL
Worcestershire sauce	1 tbsp.	15 mL
Prepared mustard	¹/₂ tsp.	2 mL
Cooking oil	1 tbsp.	15 mL
Lean ground beef	¹/₂ lb.	250 g
Chopped onion	¹/₂ cup	125 mL

Combine beans and water in medium saucepan. Bring to a boil. Cover and simmer about 50 minutes until beans can be bitten into easily.

Add next 6 ingredients. Stir.

Heat cooking oil in frying pan. Add ground beef and onion. Scramble-fry until browned. Add to beans. Pour into bean pot or small casserole. Cover and bake in 300°F (150°C) oven for about 2¹/₂ hours. Remove cover. Bake for a few minutes more until beans are as dry as you like. Leftovers may be frozen. Serves 4.

Note: If beans are soaked overnight, cut cooking time from 50 minutes to about 35 minutes. If reheating any leftover beans, add a touch of water.

Quick as a wink to make. Makes the best crunchy toast.

All-purpose flour	3 cups	700 mL
Baking powder	2 tbsp.	30 mL
Salt	1 tsp.	5 mL
Beer, room temperature	12 oz.	350 mL

Measure flour, baking powder and salt into bowl. Stir.

Add beer. Mix and turn into greased 9 x 5 inch (23 x 12 cm) loaf pan. Bake in 350°F (180°C) oven for about 50 minutes. Freezes well. Makes 1 loaf.

Pictured on page 125.

CHEESECAKE PIE

This is best made the day before. A white pie with a white topping.

CRUST

Butter or margarine	1/3 cup	75 mL
Graham cracker crumbs	1 1/4 cups	275 mL
Granulated sugar	2 tbsp.	30 mL

FILLING

Cream cheese, softened	12 oz.	750 g
Granulated sugar	1/2 cup	125 mL
Eggs	2	2
Lemon juice	2 tbsp.	30 mL
Cream or milk	2 tbsp.	30 mL
Grated lemon rind	1 tsp.	5 mL

TOPPING

Sour cream	1 1/2 cups	375 mL
Granulated sugar	2 tbsp.	30 mL

Crust: Melt butter in small saucepan. Stir in graham crumbs and sugar. Press into 9 inch (22 cm) pie plate.

Filling: Beat cream cheese and sugar together until smooth. Beat in eggs 1 at a time using medium speed. Add lemon juice, cream and lemon rind. Mix. Pour into pie shell. Bake in 350°F (180°C) oven about 20 to 30 minutes until firm.

Topping: Stir sour cream and sugar together in small bowl. Spread over top. Return to oven for 12 to 15 minutes. Cool then chill overnight. Leftovers may be frozen. Cuts into 6 to 8 wedges.

SIMPLE STRAWBERRIES

Although this may be simple, it is a classy dessert served in many restaurants.

Fresh whole strawberries	24-32	24-32
Granulated sugar	1/2 cup	125 mL
Yogurt (or sour cream)	1 cup	250 mL

Place 6 to 8 strawberries on one side of each of 4 salad plates. Spoon 2 tbsp. (30 mL) sugar beside strawberries and 1/4 cup (50 mL) yogurt beside sugar. To eat berries, dip them first in sugar then in yogurt. Serves 4.

Pictured on cover.

Crisp rice cereal is the foundation for this cool ice cream dessert.

Large marshmallows	32	32
Butter or margarine	3 tbsp.	50 mL
Brown sugar, packed	½ cup	125 mL
Crisp rice cereal	5 cups	1.12 L
SAUCE		
Brown sugar, packed	¾ cup	175 mL
Butter	6 tbsp.	100 mL
Milk	3 tbsp.	50 mL
Brandy flavoring	1 tsp.	5 mL
FRUIT TOPPING		
Raspberries	1 cup	250 mL
Ice cream scoops, your favorite flavor	4	4
Banana, sliced	1	1
Sweetened peach slices	8-12	8-12
Blueberries	8-12	8-12

Melt marshmallows, butter and brown sugar in double boiler. Stir often.

Measure rice cereal into large bowl. Pour marshmallow mixture over top. Stir well to coat. Pack into greased 8 inch (20 cm) round layer pan. Let stand until firm.

Sauce: Combine all 4 ingredients in small saucepan over medium heat. Bring to a boil. Simmer for 1 minute. Cool.

Filling: Turn out cereal base onto serving plate. Cut into wedges and put 1 on each of 4 dessert plates. Make an outside border with raspberries. Arrange ice cream scoops next to raspberry edge. Arrange banana and peach slices on or around each wedge. Spoon sauce over ice cream. Serves 4 to 6.

Pictured on page 53.

If your waffles are wrinkled use a waffle iron.

RUM CREAM PUFFS

Rum flavored custard fills these big tender puffs.

CREAM PUFFS

Water	½ cup	125 mL
Butter or margarine	¼ cup	60 mL
Salt	⅛ tsp.	0.5 mL
All-purpose flour	½ cup	125 mL
Eggs	2	2

FILLING

Milk	1½ cups	350 mL
Granulated sugar	6 tbsp.	100 mL
All-purpose flour	3 tbsp.	50 mL
Salt	¼ tsp.	1 mL
Eggs	2	2
Whipping cream (or ½ envelope topping)	½ cup	125 mL
Rum flavoring	½ tsp.	2 mL

Cream Puffs: Bring water to a boil in small saucepan over medium heat. Stir in butter and salt.

Add flour and stir rapidly until it leaves sides of pan and forms a ball. Remove from heat.

Add eggs 1 at a time beating until smooth. Drop into 6 equal mounds on greased baking sheet leaving room for expansion. Bake in 425°F (220°C) oven for about 30 minutes until they look dry and no drops of moisture show. Transfer to rack to cool. Cut tops almost off and spoon filling inside.

Filling: Heat milk in small saucepan over medium heat until it boils.

Meanwhile, in small bowl stir sugar, flour and salt together well. Add eggs mixing until smooth. Stir into boiling milk until it boils and thickens. Don't cook too long or it will curdle. If that happens, run it through blender. Cool well.

In another bowl beat cream until stiff. Add rum flavoring. Fold into filling. Fill cream puffs. Chill. Not recommended for freezing. Makes 6.

Pictured on page 71.

A chilled filling on a nutty crust, topped with whipped cream.

CRUST

Butter or margarine	1/2 cup	125 mL
Granulated sugar	2 tbsp.	30 mL
All-purpose flour	1 cup	250 mL
Finely chopped walnuts	1/3 cup	75 mL

FILLING

Peach flavored gelatin	2 x 3 oz.	2 x 85 g
Boiling water	1 1/2 cups	350 mL
Granulated sugar	1/3 cup	75 mL
Salt	1/8 tsp.	0.5 mL
Cold water	1 1/2 cups	350 mL
Lemon juice	1 tsp.	5 mL
Canned apricots with juice, cubed	14 oz.	398 mL

TOPPING

Whipping cream (or 1 envelope topping)	1 cup	250 mL
Granulated sugar	2 tsp.	10 mL
Vanilla	1/2 tsp.	2 mL

Grated semisweet chocolate (optional)

Crust: Melt butter in small saucepan. Stir in sugar, flour and walnuts. Press into 8 x 8 inch (20 x 20 cm) pan. Bake in 350°F (180°C) oven for 12 to 15 minutes. Cool well.

Filling: Stir gelatin into boiling water in bowl.

Stir in sugar until dissolved. Add next 4 ingredients. Stir. Chill until syrupy.

Pour thickened mixture over crust. Chill until set.

Topping: Beat cream, sugar and vanilla until stiff. Spread over top. Sprinkle with grated chocolate if desired. Cuts into 9 squares.

Pictured on page 71.

Paré Pointer

No matter where you hide the liquor he can always find it. He has a fifth sense.

COOL CHOCOLATE PIE

Now this is chocolate!

Butter or margarine, softened	¹/₂ cup	125 mL
Granulated sugar	³/₄ cup	175 mL
Semisweet chocolate chips, melted	1 cup	250 mL
Eggs	2	2
Vanilla	1 tsp.	5 mL
Baked pie pastry shell, 9 inch (22 cm) size	1	1
Whipping cream (or 1 envelope topping)	1 cup	250 mL
Granulated sugar	2 tsp.	10 mL
Vanilla	¹/₂ tsp.	2 mL
Cocoa	2 tbsp.	30 mL

Cream butter and first amount of sugar together in mixing bowl until light and fluffy.

Add melted chocolate. Beat well. Add eggs 1 at a time beating thoroughly after each. Add first amount of vanilla and mix.

Pour into pie shell. Chill several hours.

Beat cream, second amounts of sugar and vanilla and cocoa until stiff. Put dollop on each wedge or scoop over whole pie. Cuts into 6 pieces.

Pictured on page 71.

CHERRY TREAT

Unusual and delicious with a sour cream and condensed milk layer.

CRUST		
Butter or margarine	¹/₂ cup	125 mL
All-purpose flour	³/₄ cup	175 mL
Rolled oats	³/₄ cup	175 mL
FILLING		
Sweetened condensed milk (see Note)	11 oz.	300 mL
Sour cream	1 cup	250 mL
Cherry pie filling (or apple)	19 oz.	540 mL
Lemon juice	1 tsp.	5 mL
Almond flavoring	¹/₂ tsp.	2 mL
Chopped walnuts or pecans	¹/₂ cup	125 mL

(continued on next page)

Crust: Melt butter in medium size saucepan. Stir in flour and rolled oats. Pack into ungreased 9 x 13 inch (22 x 33 cm) pan.

Filling: Mix condensed milk and sour cream in bowl. Pour over crust.

Stir pie filling, lemon juice and almond flavoring together in another bowl. Spoon small dabs of pie filling here and there over top of sour cream layer.

Sprinkle with nuts. Bake in 350°F (180°C) oven for 35 to 45 minutes. Cuts into 15 pieces.

Note: Sweetened condensed milk in 14 oz. (398 mL) can may also be used.

MERINGUE PIE

Always a surprise pie. A crust of meringue and cracker crumbs with a chocolate cream filling.

Egg whites, room temperature	3	3
Cream of tartar	$1/4$ tsp.	1 mL
Granulated sugar	1 cup	250 mL
Cracker crumbs (Ritz is good)	$1/2$ cup	125 mL
Chopped walnuts or pecans	1 cup	250 mL
Vanilla	1 tsp.	5 mL
TOPPING		
Whipping cream (or 1 envelope topping)	1 cup	250 mL
Sweetened chocolate drink powder	3 tbsp.	50 mL
Cocoa (optional)	1 tbsp.	15 mL

Beat egg whites and cream of tartar until soft peaks form. Add sugar gradually, beating until stiff.

Fold in cracker crumbs, walnuts and vanilla. Spread in greased 10 inch (25 cm) pie plate, spreading well up sides. Bake in 300°F (150°C) oven about 35 to 45 minutes until dry. Cool. May be frozen at this point.

Topping: Beat cream until stiff. Add chocolate drink powder. Mix. Taste and add sifted cocoa to increase chocolate flavor if desired. Smooth over crust making center a bit higher than sides. Chill. Cuts into 6 wedges.

PEACH MELBA

What color! An easy dessert, well received.

Frozen sweetened raspberries in heavy syrup, thawed	10 oz.	284 g
Cornstarch	1 tbsp.	15 mL
Water	2 tbsp.	30 mL
Scoops of vanilla ice cream	4	4
Sweetened sliced peaches, canned, fresh or frozen	20	20

Drain and heat raspberry juice in small saucepan over medium heat until it boils.

Stir cornstarch into water then into boiling raspberry juice until it boils and thickens. Remove from heat. Mash raspberries and add to thickened juice. Stir. Cool.

Put scoop of ice cream in each sherbet or fruit nappie. Surround with 5 peach slices. Top with raspberry (melba) sauce. Serves 4.

BREAD CUSTARD PUDDING

A homey dessert with more custard than usual.

Eggs	2	2
Granulated sugar	3/4 cup	175 mL
Salt	1/4 tsp.	1 mL
Vanilla	3/4 tsp.	4 mL
Milk	2 1/2 cups	575 mL
Bread slices, cut in 1 inch (2.5 cm) squares	4	4
Raisins	2/3 cup	150 mL
Butter or margarine	1 tbsp.	15 mL

Beat eggs in small mixing bowl until frothy. Beat in sugar, salt and vanilla. Mix in milk, slowly.

Add bread and raisins. Stir with spoon to moisten. Pour into 1 1/2 quart (1.5 L) casserole.

Dab butter over top. Set in pan of hot water. Bake uncovered in 350°F (180°C) oven for 1 to 1 1/4 hours until firm. Leftovers may be frozen. Serves 4 to 6.

CHUNKY ANGEL IN CHOCOLATE

Melted chocolate amidst small pieces of white angel food cake.

White angel food cake, 10 inch (25 cm), cut bite size	1	1
Semisweet chocolate chips	2 cups	500 mL
Butter or margarine	2 tbsp.	30 mL
Whipping cream (or 2 envelopes topping)	2 cups	500 mL
Whipping cream (or 1 envelope topping)	1 cup	250 mL
Granulated sugar	2 tsp.	10 mL
Vanilla	1 tsp.	5 mL
Sliced almonds, toasted	3 tbsp.	50 mL

Place 1/2 of the cake pieces in ungreased 10 inch (25 cm) spring form pan.

Melt chocolate chips and butter in heavy saucepan over low heat. Stir often to hasten melting. Remove from heat. Cool.

Beat first amount of cream until stiff. Fold cream into chocolate, small amounts at a time until all is added and mixture is smooth. Spoon half of mixture over cake in pan. Cover with second half of cake pieces followed by remaining chocolate mixture. Chill.

Beat second amount of cream, sugar and vanilla until stiff. Spread over top.

Toast almonds in 350°F (180°C) oven, about 5 to 10 minutes until golden brown. Watch carefully. Sprinkle on top of dessert. Chill. Cut into wedges to serve. Leftovers may be frozen. Makes 10 servings.

PERKY RICE

Similar to fried rice without the frying.

Long grain rice	1 1/2 cups	375 mL
Finely diced carrot	1/2 cup	125 mL
Finely diced celery	1/2 cup	125 mL
Finely diced onion	1/4 cup	60 mL
Water	3 cups	750 mL
Salt	1 tsp.	5 mL

Place all ingredients in medium size heavy saucepan. Cover and bring to a boil. Boil slowly about 15 minutes until rice is tender and water is absorbed. Leftovers may be frozen. Serves 4.

Pictured on page 53.

RASPBERRY DELIGHT PIE

Absolutely divine! This may also be served from a pretty bowl instead of a pie shell. Garnish with fresh raspberries if in season.

Frozen raspberries in heavy syrup, thawed and drained, juice reserved	15 oz.	425 g
Raspberry flavored gelatin	3 oz.	85 g
Boiling water	³/₄ cup	175 mL
Raspberry juice plus water to make	³/₄ cup	175 mL
Whipping cream (or 1 envelope topping	1 cup	250 mL
Baked pie pastry shell, 9 inch (22 cm) size	1	1

Place raspberries in small bowl and reserve juice in measuring cup.

Pour raspberry gelatin into medium size bowl. Add boiling water. Stir to dissolve.

Add raspberry juice and raspberries. Stir. Chill until syrupy.

Beat cream until stiff. Fold into thickened mixture.

Pour into pie shell. Chill. Cuts into 6 pieces.

Pictured on page 71.

Keep a white or lemon angel food cake in the freezer so you can fancy it up with this frosting.

Granulated sugar	1/3 cup	75 mL
Cornstarch	2 tbsp.	30 mL
Crushed pineapple with juice	14 oz.	398 mL
Maraschino cherries, quartered	1/3 cup	75 mL
Almond flavoring	1/2 tsp.	2 mL
Unflavored gelatin	1 x 1/4 oz.	1 x 7 g
Cold water	1/3 cup	75 mL
Cold milk	2/3 cup	150 mL
Whipping cream (or 1 envelope topping)	1 cup	250 mL
White angel food cake, 10 inch (25 cm) size	1	1
Sliced almonds, toasted	2 tbsp.	30 mL

Stir sugar and cornstarch together in medium saucepan. Add pineapple with juice, cherries and almond flavoring. Heat and stir until it boils and thickens. Cool thoroughly.

Sprinkle gelatin powder over water in small saucepan. Let stand for 5 minutes. Heat and stir to dissolve gelatin. Remove from heat.

Add milk and stir. Chill until syrupy. Fold into fruit mixture.

Beat cream until stiff. Fold into thickened mixture. Spread over top and sides of cake.

Toast almonds in 350°F (180°C) oven, about 5 to 10 minutes until golden brown. Watch carefully. Sprinkle over cake. Chill. Serves 4 with lots to spare.

When asked whatever happened to his broken banjo strings he said it was a gut reaction.

MENU ONE

Meaty Chili   page 84
Dressed Greens   page 79
Pickles
Croissants   page 79
Black Forest Bowl   page 83
Coffee   Tea

MENU TWO

Beef Barley Soup   page 77
Crackers
Egg Sandwiches   page 80
Pickles
Rhubarb Crumble   page 81
Coffee   Tea

MENU THREE

Lasagne   page 75
Best Dressed Salad   page 76
Pickles
Onion Biscuits   page 76
Banana Chiffon Cake   page 85
Coffee   Tea

MENU FOUR

Broiled Buns   page 83
Vegetable Soup   page 122
Crackers
Sweet Pickles, Dill Pickles
Creamed Peaches   page 80
Coffee   Tea

MENU FIVE

Sloppy Joes   page 78
Coleslaw   page 77
Sweet Pickles, Dill Pickles
Cottage Pudding   page 82
Coffee   Tea

Make half of this recipe in a smaller pan to serve four or double the recipe using two pans to serve sixteen. Leftovers freeze and reheat well.

Cooking oil	1 tbsp.	15 mL
Ground beef	1½ lb.	750 g
Chopped onion	1½ cups	375 mL
Canned tomatoes	28 oz.	796 mL
Envelope spaghetti-sauce mix	1½ oz.	42.5 g
Garlic powder	¼ tsp.	1 mL
Eggs	2	2
Cottage cheese	2 cups	500 mL
Lasagne noodles	½ lb.	250 g
Boiling water	2½ qts.	3 L
Cooking oil	1 tbsp.	15 mL
Salt	2 tsp.	10 mL
Grated mozzarella cheese	4 cups	1 L
Grated Parmesan cheese	½ cup	125 mL

Heat cooking oil in frying pan. Add ground beef and onion. Scramble-fry until browned.

Add tomatoes, spaghetti-sauce mix and garlic powder. Simmer, stirring occasionally, for 25 to 30 minutes.

Break eggs into bowl. Spoon beat then add cottage cheese. Set aside.

Cook lasagne noodles in boiling water, cooking oil and salt in large uncovered Dutch oven about 14 to 16 minutes until tender but firm. Drain.

To assemble, layer in greased 9 × 13 inch (22 × 33 cm) pan as follows:

1. Layer of noodles
2. ⅓ cottage cheese
3. ⅓ meat sauce
4. ⅓ mozzarella cheese
5-8. and 9-12. Repeat steps 1-4
13. Sprinkle with Parmesan cheese

Bake uncovered in 350°F (180°C) oven 45 to 55 minutes. Allow about 10 minutes extra if chilled. Let stand 10 minutes before cutting. Freezes well. Serves 8.

BEST DRESSED SALAD

A dark green salad with a yummy dressing.

DRESSING

Cooking oil	1 tbsp.	15 mL
Vinegar	2 tbsp.	30 mL
Ketchup	4 tsp.	20 mL
Granulated sugar	2½ tbsp.	35 mL
Dry onion flakes	1½ tsp.	7 mL

SALAD

Romaine lettuce, torn or cut up, lightly packed	4 cups	1 L
Hard boiled eggs, chopped	2	2
Green onions, chopped	2	2

Dressing: Mix all 5 ingredients in small bowl to dissolve sugar. Chill for several hours or overnight. Makes ⅓ cup (75 mL).

Salad: Combine lettuce, egg and onion in large bowl. Just before serving add dressing and toss. Serves 4.

Note: If there is no time to chill dressing before using, substitute ⅛ tsp. (0.5 mL) onion powder in place of onion flakes.

ONION BISCUITS

The onion flavor comes from dry onion soup mix. So easy.

All-purpose flour	2 cups	450 mL
Granulated sugar	1 tbsp.	15 mL
Baking powder	4 tsp.	20 mL
Salt	½ tsp.	2 mL
Onion soup mix (envelope)	½	½
Butter or margarine, softened	⅓ cup	75 mL
Milk	¾ cup	175 mL

Combine all ingredients in bowl. Be sure to stir soup mix well before dividing in half. Mix until it forms soft ball. Pat or roll ¾ inch (2 cm) thick on lightly floured board. Cut into 1¾ inch (4.5 cm) circles. Arrange on ungreased baking sheet. Bake in 425°F (220°C) oven about 12 to 15 minutes, until risen and browned. Freezes well. Makes about 16.

BEEF BARLEY SOUP

A meaty soup. Make a big double batch and freeze whatever is left.

Cooking oil	1 tbsp.	15 mL
Round steak or stew meat, diced	1/2 lb.	250 g
Barley	3 tbsp.	50 mL
Beef bouillon cube	1 x 1/5 oz.	1 x 6 g
Bay leaf	1/2	1/2
Salt	1/2 tsp.	2 mL
Pepper	1/8 tsp.	0.5 mL
Water	5 cups	1.12 L
Diced onion	1/2 cup	125 mL
Thinly sliced carrot (or diced)	1/2 cup	125 mL
Parsley flakes	1/2 tsp.	2 mL
Diced potato	1/2 cup	125 mL

Heat cooking oil in large saucepan. Add diced steak and brown well.

Add next 6 ingredients. Cover and simmer slowly for 2 hours.

Add onion, carrot and parsley. Cook for 20 minutes.

Add potato and cook until tender. Remove bay leaf. Check for salt and pepper adding more if needed. Makes $5\frac{1}{3}$ cups (1.12 L). Freezes well. Serves 4.

Pictured on page 125.

COLESLAW

Flexible and fast if you have cabbage on hand. Multiply recipe as necessary.

Grated cabbage, packed	3 cups	750 mL
Medium grated carrot	1	1
Dry onion flakes	2 tsp.	10 mL
Cole slaw dressing (commercial type)	1/2 cup	125 mL
Celery seed, sprinkle		

Combine cabbage, carrot and onion flakes in bowl.

Pour coleslaw dressing over salad. Stir well. Sprinkle with celery seed. Stir again. Serves 4.

SLOPPY JOES

If you want to be prepared for sixteen people, simply multiply this by four. Freezing leftovers couldn't be easier.

Cooking oil	1 tbsp.	15 mL
Ground beef	1 lb.	500 g
Chopped onion	1 cup	250 mL
Chopped green pepper (optional)	2 tbsp.	30 mL
All-purpose flour	2 tbsp.	30 mL
Tomato sauce	7$\frac{1}{2}$ oz.	213 mL
Water	1$\frac{1}{3}$ cups	325 mL
Worcestershire sauce	1$\frac{1}{2}$ tsp.	7 mL
Vinegar	1$\frac{1}{2}$ tsp.	7 mL
Brown sugar	1$\frac{1}{2}$ tsp.	7 mL
Salt	1 tsp.	5 mL
Pepper	$\frac{1}{4}$ tsp.	1 mL
Prepared mustard	$\frac{1}{4}$ tsp.	1 mL
Hamburger buns, halved, and toasted	4	4

Heat cooking oil in frying pan. Scramble-fry ground beef, onion and green pepper.

Sprinkle with flour and mix well. Stir in tomato sauce and water until it boils and thickens. Turn into large heavy saucepan.

Add next 6 ingredients. Stir. Simmer gently, uncovered, stirring often for 10 to 15 minutes. Add more water if too thick.

Hamburger buns may be toasted by placing cut side down in hot frying pans until browned or may be broiled cut side up. Butter if desired. Spoon meat mixture over 2 bun halves on each plate. Freezes well. Serves 4.

Does anyone know when the first white Dalmation was spotted?

Easy last minute croissants flavored with cheese and seasoned salt.

Packaged refrigerator crescent dinner rolls (8 per carton)	1	1
Milk	2 tsp.	10 mL
Seasoned salt	1/8 tsp.	0.5 mL
Grated Parmesan cheese	1/4 cup	50 mL

Spread out crescent dough. Cut each section in half lengthwise and crosswise.

Brush each strip with milk on top side.

Mix seasoned salt and Parmesan cheese in small bowl. Sprinkle over dough. Beginning at wide edge roll toward center. Bring ends together and twist over each other similar to a pretzel. Arrange on ungreased cookie sheet. Bake in 375°F (190°C) oven for 10 to 12 minutes or until browned. Leftovers may be frozen. Makes 8.

Pictured on page 125.

DRESSED GREENS

The cucumber dressing adds good flavor to these greens.

CUCUMBER DRESSING		
Peeled and diced cucumber	1/2 cup	125 mL
Sour cream	1/3 cup	75 mL
Lemon juice	1 tsp.	5 mL
Parsley flakes	1/4 tsp.	1 mL
Dill weed	1/4 tsp.	1 mL
Salt	1/4 tsp.	1 mL
SALAD		
Head lettuce, cut bite size, lightly packed	4 cups	1L
Fresh mushrooms, sliced	8-12	8-12
Tomato slices, diced	4	4
Chives	1 tsp.	5 mL

Cucumber Dressing: Stir all 6 ingredients together in small bowl.

Salad: In large bowl combine lettuce, mushrooms, tomato and chives. Pour dressing over salad. Toss to coat. Serves 4.

SCRAMBLED EGG SANDWICHES

A wonderful last minute sandwich. A family favorite. Accent with cheese and ketchup. My children always preferred ketchup only.

Bread slices, buttered	8	8
Process cheese spread		
Ketchup		
Butter or margarine	1 tbsp.	15 mL
Eggs	6	6
Water	3 tbsp.	50 mL
Salt, sprinkle		
Pepper, sprinkle		

Lay bread slices on counter. Spread 2 slices with cheese and 2 with ketchup. You may choose to use just cheese or just ketchup.

Heat butter in frying pan. Add eggs and water. Break yolks and stir until eggs are cooked but not dry. Sprinkle with salt and pepper. Spread on 4 bread slices and cover 2 with cheese and 2 with ketchup. Cut in half. Place 1 cheese and 1 ketchup portion on each plate or 2 of the same if desired. Not recommended for freezing. Serves 4 people, 1 sandwich each.

CREAMED PEACHES

A mouth-watering creation.

Butter or margarine	2 tbsp.	30 mL
Vanilla pudding and pie filling, 6 serving size (not instant)	1	1
All-purpose flour	³/₄ cup	175 mL
Egg	1	1
Reserved peach juice		
Milk	³/₄ cup	175 mL
Canned sliced peaches, drained	14 oz.	398 mL
Cream cheese, softened	8 oz.	250 g
Granulated sugar	¹/₂ cup	125 mL

(continued on next page)

Melt butter in 9 x 13 inch (22 x 33 cm) pan.

Mix next 5 ingredients until smooth. Pour over butter in pan.

Arrange peach slices evenly on top.

Beat cream cheese and sugar together until smooth. Spoon in dabs here and there to cover peaches. Bake in 350°F (180°C) oven for about 45 minutes. Cuts into 12 to 15 pieces.

RHUBARB CRUMBLE

Be sure to keep some rhubarb in your freezer so you can make this spring dessert any time of year. Yummy.

Butter or margarine	½ cup	125 mL
All-purpose flour	1½ cups	375 mL
Rolled oats	1½ cups	375 mL
Brown sugar, packed	1 cup	250 mL
Rhubarb, cut in 1 inch (2.5 cm) lengths	5 cups	1.25 L
Water	1 cup	250 mL
Granulated sugar	1 cup	250 mL
Cornstarch	2 tbsp.	30 mL
Vanilla	1 tsp.	5 mL

Melt butter in medium saucepan. Stir in flour, rolled oats and brown sugar. Press half of this into ungreased 9 x 9 inch (22 x 22 cm) pan.

Arrange rhubarb over top.

Stir water, sugar, cornstarch and vanilla together in separate saucepan over medium heat until it boils and thickens. Pour over rhubarb. Cover with remaining crumbs. Bake in 350°F (180°C) oven about 45 minutes until cooked and browned. Cuts into 9 pieces. Leftovers may be frozen.

COTTAGE PUDDING

Serve four to sixteen with this dessert. Any not used can be iced and eaten as cake. Great for those uncertain times.

WHITE CAKE

All-purpose flour	3 cups	700 mL
Granulated sugar	1½ cups	350 mL
Baking powder	1 tbsp.	15 mL
Salt	1 tsp.	5 mL
Butter or margarine, softened	¾ cup	175 mL
Eggs	3	3
Milk	1½ cups	350 mL
Vanilla	1 tsp.	5 mL

Measure all ingredients in order given into mixing bowl. Beat on low speed until moistened. Beat at medium speed about 2 to 3 minutes until smooth. Pour into greased 9 × 13 inch (22 × 33 cm) pan. Bake in 350°F (180°C) oven about 35 to 40 minutes until an inserted wooden pick comes out clean. Cuts into 15 to 18 pieces. Spoon Brown Sugar Sauce over each serving. Leftover cake may be frozen.

BROWN SUGAR SAUCE

Brown sugar, packed	1¾ cups	400 mL
All-purpose flour	⅓ cup	75 mL
Salt	¾ tsp.	4 mL
Water	3 cups	700 mL
Vanilla	1½ tsp.	7 mL
Butter or margarine (optional)	1 tbsp.	15 mL

Combine brown sugar, flour and salt in heavy medium saucepan. Mix thoroughly.

Stir in water. Bring to a boil over medium-low heat. Stir often. A whisk will remove lumps, if any.

Add vanilla and butter. Stir. Cover and keep hot. Leftover sauce may be frozen. Makes 4 cups (900 mL).

Use part of the cake for this dessert. Ice the remaining cake for later. Extra plates can be made in no time. Serves sixteen with no extra fuss.

Chocolate cake, cut in chunks (about ¼ cake)	**3 cups**	**750 mL**
Kirsh or sherry, sprinkle (optional)		
Canned cherry pie filling	**½ x 19 oz.**	**½ x 540 mL**
Whipping cream (or ½ envelope topping)	**½ cup**	**125 mL**
Granulated sugar	**1 tsp.**	**5 mL**
Vanilla	**¼ tsp.**	**1 mL**
Coarsley grated chocolate, for garnish		
Maraschino cherries, for garnish	**4-8**	**4-8**

Place chunks of cake in pretty bowl. Sprinkle generously with kirsh. Spoon ½ can cherry pie filling over top.

Beat cream, sugar and vanilla in small bowl until stiff. Use more cream if you like lots. Spoon over cherry filling.

If desired garnish with grated chocolate and top with cherries. Chill until needed. Leftovers can be frozen. Serves 4.

Pictured on page 71.

Be sure to keep a supply of hamburger buns and bacon in the freezer for those unexpected, as well as expected, lunches.

Bacon slices	**2 lbs.**	**900 g**
Process cheese spread		
Hamburger buns, cut in half horizontally		

Fry bacon ahead of time. Cook until almost done but still soft.

Smooth process cheese spread over bun halves. Cut bacon into ½ inch (12 mm) pieces. Arrange pieces over each bun on top of cheese. About ½ slice bacon should do one half bun. Place on tray. Broil until buns brown around edges and are bubbly hot. Allow 2 buns (4 halves) per person. Cut bacon as you need it. Freeze leftover bacon for later use. May be served with soup and/or salad, depending on appetites. Serves up to 16.

MEATY CHILI

Just use what you need and freeze the rest. Double recipe to feed sixteen. Contains vegetables.

Butter or margarine	2 tbsp.	30 mL
Chopped onion	1 cup	250 mL
Green pepper, chopped	1	1
Ground beef	2¹/₂ lbs.	1.14 kg
Sliced mushrooms, drained	10 oz.	284 mL
Kidney beans, drained	2 × 14 oz.	2 × 398 mL
Kernel corn	12 oz.	341 mL
Tomato sauce	3 × 7¹/₂ oz.	3 × 213 mL
Chili powder	1 tbsp.	15 mL
Granulated sugar	1 tbsp.	15 mL
Garlic salt	¹/₄ tsp.	1 mL
Pepper	¹/₄ tsp.	1 mL
Salt	2 tsp.	10 mL
Peas	2 cups	500 mL

Melt butter in large, heavy saucepan. Add onion and green pepper. Sauté until onion is clear and soft.

Add ground beef. Stir to break up. Brown, adding more butter if needed. Transfer to large saucepan.

Add next 9 ingredients to saucepan. Bring to a boil. Simmer covered 15 minutes.

Add peas and simmer about 5 minutes more. Freezes well. Serves 8

Pictured on page 35.

Actually it should be no surprise when your back gets stiff as a board. That's your lumbar section.

Makes a large cake. Delicate banana flavor with a light texture. Serve alone, with ice cream or with canned fruit.

All-purpose flour	2 cups	500 mL
Granulated sugar	1 1/2 cups	375 mL
Baking powder	1 tbsp.	15 mL
Salt	1 tsp.	5 mL
Cooking oil	1/2 cup	125 mL
Egg yolks	7	7
Mashed ripe banana	1 cup	250 mL
Lemon juice	1 tbsp.	15 mL
Water	1 tbsp.	15 mL
Vanilla	1 tsp.	5 mL
Egg whites, room temperature	7	7
Cream of tartar	1/2 tsp.	2 mL

Sift first 4 ingredients into bowl. Make a well in center.

Measure next 6 ingredients into well. Don't beat yet. Set aside.

Beat egg whites until frothy. Add cream of tartar. Beat until very stiff. Using same beaters, beat yolk-flour mixture until smooth. Gently and gradually fold into egg whites. Turn into ungreased 10 inch (30 cm) tube pan. Bake in 325°F (160°C) oven for 60 to 65 minutes until an inserted wooden pick comes out clean. Invert pan until cake has cooled. May be frozen at this point. Ice with Brown Sugar Glaze when ready to eat.

BROWN SUGAR GLAZE

Butter or margarine	2 tbsp.	30 mL
Brown sugar, packed	1/2 cup	125 mL
Water	2 tbsp.	30 mL
Vanilla	1/2 tsp.	2 mL
Icing (confectioner's) sugar	1 cup	225 mL

Beat butter, brown sugar and water together in small bowl to dissolve sugar.

Mix in vanilla and icing sugar. Beat until smooth. If needed, add a bit of water to make a barely pourable mixture. Apply light glaze to cake. Serves 16.

MENU ONE

Crab And Noodles   page 96
Tomato Aspic   page 87
Asparagus Marinade   page 91
Garlic Toast   page 117
Rum Nut Squares   page 98
Coffee   Tea

MENU TWO

Beef And Noodles   page 97
Grapefruit Mold   page 93
Orange Biscuits   page 87
Baked Syrup   page 95
Lemon Sauce   page 128
Coffee   Tea

MENU THREE

Meat Sauced Noodles   page 92
Orange Almond Salad   page 88
Sticky Cheese Biscuits   page 91
Blueberry Cobbler   page 96
Coffee   Tea

MENU FOUR

Noodles With Steak Sauce   page 94
Dinner Rolls
Butterscotch Pudding   page 95
Strawberry Topping
Whipped Cream
Coffee   Tea

ORANGE BISCUITS

These freshly baked biscuits have a delicate orange flavor.

All-purpose flour	2 cups	450 mL
Baking powder	1 tbsp.	15 mL
Salt	1/2 tsp.	2 mL
Cold butter or margarine	3 tbsp.	50 mL
Grated orange rind	1 tbsp.	15 mL
Milk	3/4 cup	175 mL

Measure flour, baking powder and salt into bowl. Cut in butter until crumbly.

Add orange rind and milk. Mix to form soft ball. Knead 6 to 8 times. Pat or roll 3/4 inch (2 cm) thick. Cut straight down with 1 3/4 inch (4.5 cm) cookie cutter. Arrange on ungreased baking sheet. Bake in 425°F (220°C) oven about 12 to 15 minutes until risen and browned. Freezes well. Makes about 16.

TOMATO ASPIC

A dramatic red to jazz up your plate. Perfect to serve with a bland colored dish such as pasta.

Tomato juice	1 2/3 cups	375 mL
Lemon flavored gelatin	3 oz.	85 g
Seasoned salt	1/2 tsp.	2 mL
Worcestershire sauce	1 tsp.	5 mL
Cucumber, peeled, seeds removed, finely diced	1/3 cup	75 mL
Finely diced celery	1/4 cup	50 mL
Alfalfa sprouts	4 oz.	125 g
Salad dressing (or mayonnaise)		

Measure first 4 ingredients into medium size saucepan. Heat and stir over medium heat until gelatin is dissolved. Chill until syrupy.

Fold in cucumber and celery. Pour into 3 cup (750 mL) mold or individual molds. Chill.

Make a bed of alfalfa sprouts a little larger than each mold. If using larger mold make larger bed. Unmold salad over top. Put dollop of salad dressing over top or garnish with broccoli florets and green onion. Serves 4.

Pictured on page 89.

ORANGE ALMOND SALAD

A terrific side dish. Contains shrimp.

DRESSING		
Peach yogurt	¼ cup	60 mL
Sour cream	¼ cup	60 mL
Lemon juice	1 tsp.	5 mL

SALAD		
Head of curly leaf lettuce, torn, lightly packed, about 5 to 6 cups (1.1 to 1.4 mL)	1	1
Canned cocktail or small shrimp, drained	4 oz.	113 g
Canned mandarin oranges, drained, reserve juice	10 oz.	284 mL
Toasted sliced almonds	¼ cup	60 mL

Dressing: Mix all 3 ingredients in large bowl.

Salad: Add lettuce to dressing in bowl. Toss. Divide among 4 plates or bowls.

Divide shrimp among plates, placing on top of lettuce. Scatter orange segments over top. Almonds should be toasted in 350°F (180°C) oven for about 5 to 10 minutes stirring once or twice and cooled. Sprinkle salad with almonds. Serves 4.

ASPARAGUS MARINADE

A mild pickle flavor.

Canned asparagus tips, drained	12 oz.	341 mL
Italian dressing to cover		
Pimiento strips	4	4

Place asparagus spears in loaf pan. Cover with dressing. Cover pan and refrigerate to marinate for 24 hours.

Carefully lift out asparagus with slotted spoon and divide among 4 plates. Lay a strip of pimiento across spears. If you would prefer, all the spears may be arranged on one plate to place in center of table. Serves 4.

STICKY CHEESE BISCUITS

These good looking biscuits are cooked after a combination of melted butter and cheese is poured over top.

All-purpose flour	2 cups	450 mL
Baking powder	4 tsp.	20 mL
Granulated sugar	1 tsp.	5 mL
Salt	3/4 tsp.	4 mL
Cold butter or margarine	1/4 cup	60 mL
Milk	2/3 cup	150 mL
Butter or margarine	1/2 cup	125 mL
Grated medium Cheddar cheese	1 cup	250 mL

Measure first 4 ingredients into bowl. Cut in butter until crumbly.

Stir in milk until it forms a ball of soft dough. Knead 6 to 8 times. Roll or pat dough 3/4 inch (2 cm) thick. Cut straight down with 1 3/4 inch (4.5 cm) round cookie cutter. Arrange in ungreased 8 x 8 inch (20 x 20 cm) shallow pan. Line with foil for easy clean-up.

Melt butter and then cool. Add cheese. Stir and then spoon over each biscuit. Bake in 425°F (220°C) oven for 12 to 15 minutes. Makes about 16.

Pictured on page 125.

MEAT SAUCED NOODLES

A plateful of pasta covered with a meat sauce. Not a red sauce.

MEAT SAUCE

Cooking oil	1½ tbsp.	25 mL
Ground beef	1½ lbs.	700 g
Chopped onion	¾ cup	175 mL
All-purpose flour	3 tbsp.	50 mL
Salt	1½ tsp.	7 mL
Pepper, generous measure	¼ tsp.	1 mL
Beef bouillon powder	1 tsp.	5 mL
Garlic powder	¼ tsp.	1 mL
Condensed cream of mushroom soup	10 oz.	284 mL
Sour cream	1 cup	250 mL
Noodles, medium or broad	13 oz.	375 g
Boiling water	4 qts.	5 L
Cooking oil	1 tbsp.	15 mL
Salt	1 tbsp.	15 mL

Meat Sauce: Heat first amount of cooking oil in frying pan. Add ground beef and onion. Scramble-fry until browned.

Mix in flour, first amount of salt, pepper, bouillon powder and garlic powder. Stir in soup and sour cream until it boils and thickens. Keep hot while noodles cook.

Cook noodles in boiling water, second amounts of cooking oil and salt in large uncovered saucepan about 5 to 7 minutes until tender but firm. Drain. Arrange on 4 plates. Cover with sauce. Noodles and sauce may be served separately if you like. Leftovers may be frozen. Serves 4.

If your dog keeps yipping while out walking, your best bet is to take it to a barking lot.

A shimmering citrus beauty.

Unflavored gelatin	1 x ¼ oz.	1 x 7 g
Water	¼ cup	50 mL
Granulated sugar	½ cup	125 mL
Drained grapefruit juice	1¼ cups	275 mL
Canned grapefruit sections, drained	14 oz.	398 mL
Canned mandarin oranges, drained	10 oz.	284 mL
Chopped celery	½ cup	125 mL
Chopped maraschino cherries	2 tbsp.	30 mL
DRESSING		
Salad dressing (or mayonnaise)	¼ cup	60 mL
Lime juice	1 tbsp.	15 mL
Granulated sugar	4 tsp.	20 mL
Whipping cream	¼ cup	60 mL

Sprinkle gelatin over water in small saucepan. Let stand 5 minutes. Heat and stir to dissolve gelatin.

Stir in sugar to dissolve. Add grapefruit juice. Pour into bowl. Chill until syrupy.

Fold in grapefruit, orange, celery and cherries. Pour into 4 cup (1 L) mold. Chill. Unmold. Serve with dressing.

Dressing: Stir salad dressing, lime juice and sugar in medium bowl.

Beat cream until stiff. Fold into salad dressing mixture. Unmold salad and top with dressing. Serves 4 amply.

Variation: Fresh fruit and juice may be used in place of canned.

Paré Pointer

She thinks a drive-in restaurant is the place to go if you are trying to curb your appetite.

NOODLES WITH STEAK SAUCE

Economy steak in a tomato cream sauce!

STEAK SAUCE

Cooking oil	1 tbsp.	15 mL
Round steak or stew meat, diced	1 lb.	500 g
Chopped onion	1 cup	250 mL
Salt	1 tsp.	5 mL
Pepper	¼ tsp.	1 mL
Water	1 cup	250 mL
All-purpose flour	1 tbsp.	15 mL
Tomato sauce	7½ oz.	213 mL
Sour cream	½ cup	125 mL
Red wine (or alcohol-free wine)	1 tbsp.	15 mL
Medium width noodles	13 oz.	375 g
Boiling water	4 qts.	5 L
Cooking oil	1 tbsp.	15 mL
Salt	1 tbsp.	15 mL

Steak Sauce: Heat first amount of cooking oil in heavy saucepan. Add meat and brown all sides well.

Add onion, first amount of salt, pepper and water. Bring to a boil. Simmer covered about 1½ hours until very tender. Add more water as needed but try not to have much left when meat is cooked.

Whisk flour in tomato sauce until smooth. Stir into meat along with sour cream and wine. Bring to a boil briefly. Keep hot while noodles cook.

In large uncovered saucepan cook noodles in boiling water, second amounts of cooking oil and salt until tender but firm, about 5 to 7 minutes. Drain. Divide among 4 plates. Divide meat sauce over top. If you like, noodles and meat sauce can be served separately. Leftovers may be frozen. Serves 4.

Paré Pointer

There was soup on the menu until the waiter wiped it off.

This old family favorite is an odd combination but a good one. Canned or frozen strawberries work equally well over this.

Butterscotch pudding powder, 4 serving size (not instant)	1	1
Frozen sliced strawberries, thawed, or canned strawberries	½ cup	125 mL
Whipping cream (or ½ envelope topping)	½ cup	125 mL
Granulated sugar	1 tsp.	5 mL
Vanilla	½ tsp.	2 mL

Prepare pudding as directed on package. Chill.

Spoon chilled pudding into 4 sherbets. Spoon some berries and juice over top.

Beat cream, sugar and vanilla in small bowl until almost stiff. Put dollop on each. Serves 4.

BAKED SYRUP

This is like a cake when baked. It's scrumptious with a lemon sauce.

Corn syrup	1 cup	250 mL
Butter or margarine, softened	2 tbsp.	30 mL
Egg	1	1
All purpose flour	1¼ cups	300 mL
Baking powder	½ tsp.	2 mL
Baking soda	½ tsp.	2 mL
Salt	½ tsp.	2 mL

Combine syrup, butter and egg in mixing bowl. Beat well.

Add remaining ingredients. Mix well. Turn into greased 8 x 8 inch (20 x 20 cm) pan. Bake in 350°F (180°C) oven about 30 minutes until an inserted wooden pick comes out clean . Let stand 20 minutes. Remove from pan. Serve warm with warm Lemon Sauce, page 128, over each serving. Serves 4 to 6.

BLUEBERRY COBBLER

A moist pudding that pleases all kinds of appetites.

Blueberry pie filling	19 oz.	540 mL
Lemon juice	1 tsp.	5 mL
All-purpose flour	1 cup	250 mL
Granulated sugar	3 tbsp.	50 mL
Baking powder	1½ tsp.	7 mL
Salt	½ tsp.	2 mL
Cold butter or margarine	3 tbsp.	50 mL
Cold milk	½ cup	125 mL

Measure pie filling and lemon juice into bowl. Stir. Turn into 8 inch (20 cm) casserole. Place in hot 375°F (190°C) oven while preparing topping.

Measure next 4 ingredients into bowl. Cut in butter until crumbly.

Add milk. Stir to moisten. Drop by spoonfuls to cover hot filling. Bake uncovered in 425°F (220°C) oven about 20 to 25 minutes until risen and browned. Leftovers may be frozen. Serves 4 to 6.

CRAB AND NOODLES

A terrific combination. Grated Cheddar cheese gives color as well as flavor. Leftovers may be frozen.

Broad egg noodles	3 cups	750 mL
Boiling water	2½ qts.	3 L
Cooking oil	1 tbsp.	15 mL
Salt	2 tsp.	10 mL
Butter or margarine	2 tbsp.	30 mL
Chopped onion	⅓ cup	75 mL
All-purpose flour	2 tbsp.	30 mL
Salt	½ tsp.	2 mL
Pepper	¼ tsp.	1 mL
Prepared mustard	½ tsp.	2 mL
Milk	1½ cups	375 mL
Crabmeat (or canned crab)	2 cups	500 mL
Grated medium Cheddar cheese	1¼ cups	300 mL

(continued on next page)

Cook egg noodles in boiling water, cooking oil and first amount of salt in large uncovered saucepan about 5 to 7 minutes until tender but firm. Drain. Return noodles to saucepan.

Meanwhile melt butter in another saucepan. Add onion and sauté until clear. Do not brown.

Sprinkle with flour, salt and pepper. Mix well. Stir in mustard and milk until it boils and thickens. Add half of this sauce to drained noodles. Stir. Divide among 4 small casseroles.

Divide crab over noodles. Pour remaining sauce over crab.

Sprinkle with cheese. Lay a piece of greased foil over top and bake in 350°F (180°C) oven about 20 to 25 minutes until heated through. Remove foil for about 5 minutes more, to brown. Serves 4.

Pictured on page 35.

BEEF AND NOODLES

So flavorful and cheesy.

Medium egg noodles	8 oz.	250 g
Boiling salted water	2¹/₂ qts.	3 L
Cooking oil	1 tbsp.	15 mL
Salt	2 tsp.	10 mL
Ground beef	1 lb.	454 g
Chopped onion	³/₄ cup	175 mL
Cooking oil	1 tbsp.	15 mL
Condensed cream of mushroom soup	10 oz.	284 mL
Milk	¹/₂ cup	125 mL
Salt	¹/₂ tsp.	2 mL
Seasoned salt	¹/₄ tsp.	1 mL
Pepper	¹/₈ tsp.	0.5 mL
Grated medium Cheddar cheese	1 cup	250 mL
Grated medium Cheddar cheese	1 cup	250 mL

Cook noodles in boiling salted water and first amounts of cooking oil and salt in large uncovered saucepan about 15 minutes until tender but firm. Drain. Pour noodles into 2 quart (2.5 L) casserole.

Brown beef and onion in second amount of cooking oil in frying pan.

Add next 6 ingredients to frying pan. Mix. Pour over noodles. Lift with fork here and there so some sauce penetrates.

Sprinkle with remaining cheese. Cover and bake in 350°F (180°C) oven for 20 minutes. Remove cover. Bake until hot and browned. Leftovers may be frozen. Serves 4 generously.

RUM NUT SQUARES

A good rich dessert.

CRUST		
Butter or margarine	⅓ cup	75 mL
Graham cracker crumbs	1¼ cups	275 mL
Granulated sugar	2 tbsp.	30 mL
FILLING		
Butter or margarine, softened	½ cup	125 mL
Icing (confectioner's) sugar	1½ cups	375 mL
Vanilla	1 tsp.	5 mL
Rum flavoring	¼ tsp.	1 mL
Eggs	2	2
TOPPING		
Whipping cream	½ cup	125 mL
Chopped walnuts	½ cup	125 mL
Rum flavoring	¼ tsp.	1 mL

Crust: Melt butter in saucepan. Stir in graham crumbs and sugar. Measure out ¼ cup (60 mL) and reserve. Pack remainder in ungreased 8 × 8 inch (20 × 20 cm) pan. Set aside.

Filling: Cream butter, icing sugar, vanilla and rum flavoring until smooth, adding more to taste if desired. Beat in eggs 1 at a time. Spread over crumbs.

Topping: Beat cream until stiff. Fold in walnuts. Spread over filling. Sprinkle with reserved crumbs. Chill. Cuts into 6 good size pieces.

If you pick a four-leaf clover from poison ivy, you are bound to have a rash of good luck.

MENU ONE

Ham And Asparagus Quiche   page 100
Layered Jellied Salad   page 104
Dill Biscuits   page 102
Fried Apples   page 110
Coffee   Tea

MENU TWO

Omelet Casserole   page 100
Baked Tomatoes   page 111
Buttered Toast
Oven Rice Pudding   page 111
Coffee   Tea

MENU THREE

Broccoli Quiche   page 101
Strawberry Frost Salad   page 105
Cloverleaf Rolls
Apple Cream Dessert   page 109
Coffee   Tea

MENU FOUR

Tomato Omelet   page 103
Spring Salad   page 102
Buttered Toast
Chilled Cheesecake   page 113
Coffee   Tea

MENU FIVE

Green Chili Quiche   page 106
Spinach And Apple Salad   page 110
Sliced Baguette
Fruit Compote   page 112
Chocolate Pie   page 112
Coffee   Tea

HAM AND ASPARAGUS QUICHE

These ingredients go hand in hand. Good for lunch.

Butter or margarine	1 tbsp.	15 mL
Chopped onion	½ cup	125 mL
Cooked ham, chopped	¼ lb.	125 g
Grated medium Cheddar cheese, lightly packed	1 cup	250 mL
Eggs	3	3
Light cream	1 cup	250 mL
Pepper, sprinkle		
Canned asparagus, drained	10 oz.	284 mL
Pastry lined 9 inch (22 cm) pie plate	1	1

Melt butter in frying pan or saucepan. Add onion and sauté until soft. Add ham. Continue to sauté until onions are golden.

Add cheese. Stir to melt.

Beat eggs in small mixing bowl until frothy. Slowly beat in cream and pepper. Stir egg mixture into ham mixture. Remove from heat. Cool a bit.

Arrange asparagus spears in prepared pie shell placing tops in center. Pour warm mixture over asparagus. Bake in 425°F (220°C) oven for about 30 minutes until an inserted knife comes out clean. Leftovers may be frozen. Serves 4.

OMELET CASSEROLE

At last, an omelet that cooks by itself.

Bacon slices	6	6
Fresh mushrooms, sliced	1 lb.	454 g
Green onions, sliced	4	4
Eggs	8	8
Milk	1 cup	250 mL
Salt	½ tsp.	2 mL
Pepper	⅛ tsp.	0.5 mL
Seasoned salt	⅛ tsp.	0.5 mL
Grated Monterey Jack cheese	2½ cups	600 mL

(continued on next page)

Fry bacon in frying pan. Drain on paper towels.

Sauté mushrooms and onion in frying pan. Add butter or margarine if there isn't enough bacon fat.

Beat eggs in mixing bowl until frothy. Mix in milk, salt, pepper, seasoned salt and cheese. Crumble bacon and add along with mushrooms and onion. Pour into 2 quart (2.5 L) casserole. Bake uncovered in 350°F (180°C) oven for about 35 to 40 minutes until set. Serves 6 to 8.

Pictured on page 107.

BROCCOLI QUICHE

A tasty favorite.

Butter or margarine	2 tbsp.	30 mL
Chopped onion	1 cup	250 mL
Sliced fresh mushrooms	1 cup	250 mL
All-purpose flour	2 tbsp.	30 mL
Salt	1 tsp.	5 mL
Pepper	1/4 tsp.	1 mL
Milk	1 cup	250 mL
Eggs, lightly beaten	3	3
Chopped broccoli, cooked and drained	2 cups	500 mL
Grated medium Cheddar cheese, lightly packed	1 cup	250 mL
Pastry lined 9 inch (20 cm) pie plate or 4 individual meat pie pans	1	1

Melt butter in frying pan. Add onion and mushrooms. Sauté until soft.

Mix in flour, salt and pepper. Stir in milk until it boils and thickens. Remove from heat.

Add eggs stirring briskly. Add broccoli.

Sprinkle cheese in bottom of prepared pie shell. Pour warm mixture over top. Bake on bottom shelf in 375°F (190°C) oven about 30 minutes until an inserted knife comes out clean. Leftovers may be frozen. Serves 4.

Pictured on page 107.

DILL BISCUITS

A different variation to a biscuit. A nice surprise.

All-purpose flour	2 cups	450 mL
Baking powder	4 tsp.	20 mL
Granulated sugar	1 tbsp.	15 mL
Salt	1/2 tsp.	2 mL
Grated Parmesan cheese	2 tsp.	10 mL
Parsley flakes	1 tsp.	5 mL
Onion powder	1/4 tsp.	1 mL
Dill seed	1/2 tsp.	2 mL
Milk	3/4 cup	175 mL
Cooking oil	1/3 cup	75 mL

Measure first 8 ingredients into medium size bowl. Stir.

Add milk and cooking oil. Stir to form soft ball. Pat or roll on lightly floured surface 3/4 inch (2 cm) thick. Cut straight down with 1 3/4 inch (4.5 cm) cookie cutter. Arrange on ungreased baking sheet. Bake in 425°F (220°C) oven for about 12 to 15 minutes until raised and browned. Freezes well. Makes about 16.

SPRING SALAD

A different dressing turns this into a light refreshing salad.

DRESSING		
Red wine vinegar	1 tbsp.	15 mL
Granulated sugar	1 tbsp.	15 mL
Cooking oil	2 tbsp.	30 mL
Dry mustard powder	1/4 tsp.	1 mL
SALAD		
Greens, assorted or single, cut or torn, lightly packed	4 cups	1 L
Chopped chives	1 tbsp.	15 mL
Seedless grapes, halved or whole	1 cup	250 mL
Grated medium Cheddar cheese	1/2 cup	125 mL

Dressing: Mix all 4 ingredients.

Salad: Combine greens, chives, grapes and cheese in large bowl. Pour dressing over all. Toss. Serves 4.

This cooks all by itself over low heat on top of the stove. Be sure to try the soy sauce to see how it adds to the flavor.

Bacon slices	6	6
Sliced onion	1 cup	250 mL
Sliced tomatoes	3-4	3-4
Salt, sprinkle		
Pepper, sprinkle		
Basil, light sprinkle		
Eggs	8	8
Water	2 tbsp.	30 mL
Parsley flakes	1/4 tsp.	1 mL
Salt, sprinkle		
Pepper, sprinkle		
Soy sauce, sprinkle		

Fry bacon in heavy 10 inch (25 cm) frying pan. Remove and cut each slice into bite size pieces.

Fry onion slowly in bacon fat until soft and golden brown. Drain. Spread onion evenly over frying pan.

Place layer of tomatoes over onion. Arrange bacon pieces on tomatoes. Sprinkle with first amounts of salt and pepper, and with basil.

Beat eggs, water, parsley and second amounts of salt and pepper together in bowl with fork or whisk. Pour over all. Cover and cook over as low heat as possible until eggs are set about 20 to 25 minutes.

Sprinkle with soy sauce. Cut into quarters. Serves 4.

Pictured on page 107.

Even though pancake makeup is a good product, most people still prefer syrup.

LAYERED JELLIED SALAD

Very showy with a green, yellow and orange layer. Made with raw vegetables.

Lemon flavored gelatin	3 oz.	85 g
Salt	1½ tsp.	7 mL
Boiling water	1 cup	225 mL
Cold water	½ cup	125 mL
Vinegar	1½ tbsp.	25 mL
Finely grated carrot	¾ cup	175 mL
Finely grated cabbage	1 cup	250 mL
Finely chopped broccoli	¾ cup	175 mL
Lettuce leaves	6	6
Salad dressing (or mayonnaise)		

Dissolve gelatin and salt in boiling water in small bowl.

Stir in cold water and vinegar. Divide into 3 equal parts in small bowls. Chill until syrupy.

Add carrot to 1 portion of gelatin. Mix. Pour into 6 individual jelly molds. Chill until firm but not too set. Meanwhile leave other 2 bowls of jelly at room temperature.

Add cabbage to another portion of gelatin. Mix and pour over carrot. Chill until firm but not too set.

Add broccoli to last portion of gelatin. Mix and pour over cabbage. Chill.

Unmold onto lettuce leaf. Top with dollop of salad dressing. Garnish with tiny tomato wedges and parsley. Makes 6 molds about ½ cup (125 mL) each.

Pictured on page 89.

You can always tell when two conceited people meet. It's an "I" for an "I".

STRAWBERRY FROST SALAD

Always ready in the freezer. A pretty pink color and a joy to eat.

Strawberry flavored gelatin	3 oz.	85 g
Boiling water	1 cup	225 mL
Pineapple juice, from crushed pineapple	1/2 cup	125 mL
Salad dressing (or mayonnaise)	1/2 cup	125 mL
Crushed pineapple, drained	14 oz.	398 mL
Seedless red grapes, halved	1/2 cup	125 mL
Chopped maraschino cherries	1/4 cup	50 mL
Chopped pecans or walnuts	1/4 cup	50 mL
Banana, peeled and diced	1	1
Whipping cream (or 1 envelope topping)	1 cup	250 mL
Lettuce leaves	4	4

Combine gelatin and boiling water in medium bowl. Stir to dissolve.

Whisk in pineapple juice and salad dressing. Chill until mixture begins to thicken. Stir once or twice while thickening.

Fold in pineapple, grapes, cherries, pecans and banana.

Beat cream until stiff. Fold into salad. Spoon into muffin tins lined with paper cups. Freeze uncovered. Store in covered container.

To serve remove paper cups and place 2 salads on each lettuce leaf. Garnish with pretty green leaves. Makes about 20 using large paper cups.

Pictured on cover.

The reason winters seem so long is that they come in one year and out the other.

GREEN CHILI QUICHE

Two kinds of cheese plus a mild green chili flavor. Good choice for lunch.

Pastry-lined 9 inch (22 cm) pie plate	1	1
Grated Monterey Jack cheese	1½ cups	375 mL
Grated medium Cheddar cheese	1 cup	250 mL
Canned chopped green chilies	4 oz.	114 mL
Canned mushroom pieces, drained	10 oz.	284 mL
Eggs	3	3
Salt	¼ tsp.	1 mL
Pepper	⅛ tsp.	0.5 mL
Cumin	¼ tsp.	1 mL
Milk	1 cup	250 mL
Grated medium Cheddar cheese	½ cup	125 mL

In unbaked pastry shell scatter Monterey Jack cheese, followed by first amount of Cheddar cheese, green chilies and mushrooms.

Beat eggs until frothy. Mix in salt, pepper and cumin. Add milk. Pour over mushrooms.

Sprinkle with remaining cheese. Bake on bottom shelf in 350°F (180°C) oven about 35 to 40 minutes until an inserted knife comes out clean. Leftovers may be frozen. Serves 4.

Pictured on page 107.

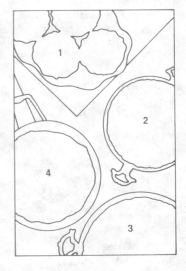

Fresh apples over a crumb crust with a creamy topping. A chilled dessert.

CRUST

Graham cracker crumbs	1¼ cups	275 mL
Granulated sugar	2 tbsp.	30 mL
Butter or margarine, melted	⅓ cup	75 mL

FILLING

Butter or margarine	1 tbsp.	15 mL
Medium apples, peeled and sliced	5	5
Cinnamon, sprinkle		
Eggs	3	3
Sour cream	1 cup	250 mL
Granulated sugar	½ cup	125 mL
Lemon juice	½ tsp.	2 mL
Vanilla	½ tsp.	2 mL
Salt	⅛ tsp.	0.5 mL

Crust: Mix graham crumbs, sugar and melted butter in small bowl. Measure and reserve 2 tbsp. (30 mL) for topping. Pack remaining crumbs into ungreased 8 x 8 inch (20 x 20 cm) pan.

Filling: Melt butter in frying pan. Add apples and sauté for 2 minutes. Cover. Simmer slowly until tender. Sprinkle with cinnamon. Cool. Pour over crust.

Beat eggs in top of double boiler. Mix in sour cream, sugar, lemon juice, vanilla and salt. Cook, stirring often, until slightly thickened. Pour over apples. Sprinkle with reserved crumbs. Chill at least 2 to 3 hours. Cuts into 9 pieces.

Paré Pointer

Did you hear about the two silkworms that were in a race? They ended up in a tie.

SPINACH AND APPLE SALAD

Sensational flavor and so pretty with red apple.

Spinach leaves torn bite size, lightly packed	5 cups	1.12 L
Bacon slices, crispy fried and crumbled	3	3
Frozen condensed orange juice, thawed	2 tbsp.	30 mL
Salad dressing (or mayonnaise)	3 tbsp.	50 mL
Small red apple, unpeeled, quartered, thinly sliced	1	1

Combine spinach and bacon in large bowl.

Stir orange juice and salad dressing together. Add apple slices. Stir to coat to prevent apple from turning brown.

Pour over spinach and bacon. Toss. Serves 4.

FRIED APPLES

A quick frying pan dessert. Can easily be increased.

Medium size cooking apples (Golden Delicious or McIntosh)	4	4
Lemon juice	2 tsp.	10 mL
Butter or margarine	2 tbsp.	30 mL
Brown sugar	2 tbsp.	30 mL
Butter or margarine	1 tbsp.	15 mL
Graham cracker crumbs	1/4 cup	50 mL
Granulated sugar	1 tsp.	5 mL

Peel apples, quarter and cut each quarter into 3 slices. Combine with lemon juice in large bowl. Toss well to coat.

Melt first amount of butter in large frying pan. Add brown sugar. Add apple and cover. Cook about 15 minutes until apples are tender, stirring occasionally. Divide among 4 bowls.

Melt second amount of butter in small saucepan. Stir in graham crumbs and sugar. Sprinkle over apple. Serves 4.

BAKED TOMATOES

When tomato slices are seasoned with parsley and basil before baking, they take on a new life.

Medium tomatoes, sliced ½ inch (12 mm) thick	7-8	7-8
Salt, sprinkle		
Pepper, sprinkle		
Butter or margarine	3 tbsp.	50 mL
Cracker crumbs	¾ cup	175 mL
Parsley flakes	¾ tsp.	4 mL
Basil	¾ tsp.	4 mL

Arrange tomato slices in single layer in greased baking pan. Sprinkle with salt and pepper.

Melt butter in small saucepan. Stir in cracker crumbs, parsley and basil. Sprinkle over tomato slices. Bake in 350°F (180°C) oven about 20 minutes until lightly browned. Do not freeze. Serves 6 to 8.

Pictured on page 53.

OVEN RICE PUDDING

A creamy pudding that needs very little watching. A real comfort food.

Milk	4 cups	1 L
Short grain rice	½ cup	125 mL
Granulated sugar	3 tbsp.	50 mL
Raisins	⅓ cup	75 mL
Vanilla	1 tsp.	5 mL
Salt	½ tsp.	2 mL
Cinnamon (optional but good)	¼ tsp.	1 mL

Combine all ingredients in 8 inch (20 cm) casserole. The addition of cinnamon is delicious although the pudding will not be as white as it would be without it. Bake in 350°F (180°C) oven for about 1½ hours until rice is soft and pudding is creamy. Stir in the skin formation at least twice during baking time. Allow skin to remain for last part of cooking. Serve warm with or without pouring cream. Leftovers can be eaten cold. Serves 6 to 8.

CHOCOLATE PIE

A smooth chocolate-marshmallow filling in a crumb crust. Sinful, I'm sure!

CRUST		
Butter or margarine	⅓ cup	60 mL
Graham cracker crumbs	1¼ cups	275 mL
Granulated sugar	2 tbsp.	30 mL

FILLING		
Milk	½ cup	125 mL
Large marshmallows	16	16
Semisweet chocolate chips	⅔ cup	150 mL
Whipping cream (or 1 envelope topping)	1 cup	250 mL
Reserved crumbs	¼ cup	50 mL
Chopped walnuts or almonds	¼ cup	50 mL

Crust: Melt butter in saucepan. Add graham crumbs and sugar. Stir well. Reserve ¼ cup (50 mL) of this mixture. Press rest into ungreased 9 inch (22 cm) pie plate to form crust.

Filling: Measure milk, marshmallows and chocolate chips into large, heavy saucepan. Stir often over low heat until melted and smooth. Cool.

In another bowl beat cream until stiff. Fold into cooled chocolate mixture. Turn into prepared crust. Smooth top.

Mix reserved crumbs and walnuts. Sprinkle over top. Chill. Cuts into 6 wedges.

FRUIT COMPOTE

Hot, colorful fruit makes a good extra to serve with quiche.

Canned fruit salad or fruit cocktail, drained	14 oz.	398 mL
Canned apricots, drained, quartered and pitted	14 oz.	398 mL
Maraschino cherries, whole or halved	8	8
Brown sugar, packed	½ cup	125 mL
Butter or margarine	¼ cup	60 mL
Curry powder	½ tsp.	2 mL

(continued on next page)

Place fruit in 1 quart (1 L) casserole.

Combine sugar, butter and curry powder in small saucepan over medium heat. Stir to melt butter. Pour over fruit. Bake uncovered in 350°F (180°C) oven about 20 minutes until hot. Use slotted spoon to serve hot. Serves 4.

CHILLED CHEESECAKE

Although this is a chilled cheesecake, it has a similar consistency to a baked one. Add your favorite topping.

CRUST		
Butter or margarine	¹/₃ **cup**	**75 mL**
Graham cracker crumbs	**1¹/₄ cups**	**275 mL**
Granulated sugar	**2 tbsp.**	**30 mL**
FILLING		
Unflavored gelatin	**1 x ¹/₄ oz.**	**1 x 7 g**
Water	⁷/₈ **cup**	**200 mL**
Cream cheese, softened	**2 x 8 oz.**	**2 x 250 g**
Granulated sugar	**1 cup**	**250 mL**
Lemon juice	**2 tbsp.**	**30 mL**
Vanilla	**1¹/₂ tsp.**	**7 mL**
Cherry, blueberry or peach pie filling or sweetened strawberries	**19 oz.**	**540 mL**

Crust: Melt butter in saucepan. Stir in graham crumbs and sugar. Press into ungreased 8 inch (20 cm) springform pan or 8 x 8 inch (20 x 20 cm) pan.

Filling: Sprinkle gelatin over water in saucepan. Let stand 5 minutes. Heat and stir until it dissolves.

Beat cream cheese, sugar, lemon juice and vanilla in mixing bowl until smooth. Slowly beat in gelatin-water mixture. Pour over crust. Chill at least 3 to 4 hours.

Cut into wedges or squares. Top with your favorite fruit topping. Cuts into 8 to 12 wedges or 9 squares.

SALADS, SANDWICHES, SOUPS

MENU ONE

Shrimp Salad   page 120
Parmesan Bread   page 121
Apple Dessert Cake   page 128
Lemon Sauce   page 128
Coffee   Tea

MENU TWO

Vegetable Soup   page 122
Chicken Salad   page 119
Cheese Biscuits   page 117
Dipped Fruit   page 118
Coffee   Tea

MENU THREE

Broccoli Cream Soup   page 115
Crackers
Toast Casimir   page 116
Apple Squares   page 129
Coffee   Tea

MENU FOUR

Shrimp Soup   page 115
Crackers
Chicken Zucchini Sandwich   page 127
Apricot Chiffon   page 116
Coffee   Tea

MENU FIVE

Exotic Soup   page 120
Crackers
Shrimp Sandwich   page 123
Gherkins
Blueberry Soufflé   page 118
Coffee   Tea

MENU SIX

Chicken Soup   page 124
Crackers
Parmesan Salad   page 122
Garlic Toast   page 117
Apple Freeze   page 128
Gingersnaps   page 121
Coffee   Tea

BROCCOLI CREAM SOUP

A simple way to make broccoli soup. Just keep frozen broccoli on hand.

Frozen chopped broccoli	10 oz.	250 g
Boiling salted water		
Milk	2 cups	500 mL
Condensed cream of mushroom soup	10 oz.	284 mL
Butter or margarine	1 tbsp.	15 mL
Salt	1 tsp.	5 mL
Pepper	1/8 tsp.	0.5 mL
Tarragon	1/8 tsp.	0.5 mL
All-purpose flour	3 tbsp.	50 mL
Water	6 tbsp.	100 mL

Cook broccoli in boiling salted water until tender. Drain.

Add next 6 ingredients. Heat and stir until mixed. Continue to heat stirring occasionally until hot. Taste for salt and pepper adding more if needed.

Whisk flour into water in small bowl until smooth. Stir into boiling soup until it returns to a boil and thickens. Freezes well. Serves 4 people a generous 1 cup (250 mL) each.

Pictured on page 125.

SHRIMP SOUP

A most pleasant way to begin a lunch. Freezes well.

Butter or margarine	3 tbsp.	50 mL
All-purpose flour	3 tbsp.	50 mL
Salt	1/2 tsp.	2 mL
Pepper	1/8 tsp.	0.5 mL
Milk	3 cups	750 mL
Canned cream style corn	1/2 cup	125 mL
Canned broken or small shrimp, rinsed and drained	4 oz.	113 g
Chopped chives	1 tsp.	5 mL

Melt butter in saucepan. Mix in flour, salt and pepper. Stir in milk until it boils and thickens.

Add remaining ingredients. Bring to the boiling point. Serves 4.

APRICOT CHIFFON

Delicate and frothy.

Canned apricots with juice, run through blender or press through sieve	14 oz.	398 mL
Granulated sugar	1/3 cup	75 mL
All-purpose flour	2 tbsp.	30 mL
Egg yolks	2	2
Water	3 tbsp.	50 mL
Lemon juice	2 tsp.	10 mL
Vanilla	1/2 tsp.	2 mL
Egg whites, room temperature	2	2

Bring apricot purée to a boil over medium heat.

Mix next 6 ingredients. Stir into boiling purée until it returns to a boil and thickens. Remove from heat.

Beat egg whites until stiff. Fold into hot mixture. Turn into serving bowl or spoon directly into sherbets. Chill. Pass pouring cream on the side. Serve with Gingersnaps, page 121. Serves 4.

TOAST CASIMIR

Very unusual. Mild and different. Excellent choice.

Butter or margarine	2 1/3 tbsp.	35 mL
All-purpose flour	2 1/3 tbsp.	35 mL
Salt	1 1/2 tsp.	7 mL
Pepper	1/4 tsp.	1 mL
Curry powder	3/4 tsp.	4 mL
Milk	3 cups	700 mL
Salad dressing (or mayonnaise)	3/4 cup	175 mL
Slivered red pepper	1/4 cup	60 mL
Currants (or cut up raisins)	3 tbsp.	50 mL
Green tipped bananas, halved lengthwise and sliced	1 1/2	1 1/2
Chopped chicken or turkey	3 cups	700 mL
Bread slices, toasted and buttered	8	8

(continued on next page)

Melt butter in large saucepan. Mix in flour, salt, pepper and curry powder. Stir in milk until it boils and thickens.

Add salad dressing and stir. Add next 4 ingredients. Mix well and heat through.

Place 1 slice of toast on each large plate with point facing front. Cut other 4 slices in half cornerwise. Place 2 halves on each plate, 1 on each side of whole slice with long sides touching side points. Spoon chicken mixture over center slice. Serves 4.

CHEESE BISCUITS

These fresh biscuits always make a meal better.

All-purpose flour	2 cups	450 mL
Baking powder	4 tsp.	20 mL
Salt	$1/2$ tsp.	2 mL
Butter or margarine	$1/4$ cup	60 mL
Grated sharp Cheddar cheese	1 cup	225 mL
Milk	$3/4$ cup	175 mL

Measure flour, baking powder, salt and butter into bowl. Cut in butter until crumbly.

Add cheese and milk. Stir to form soft ball. Add more milk if necessary. Knead 8 to 10 times on lightly floured surface. Pat or roll $3/4$ inch (2 cm) thick. Cut into $1 3/4$ inch (4.5 cm) circles or squares. Arrange on ungreased baking sheet. Bake in 425°F (220°C) oven about 12 to 15 minutes until risen and browned. Freezes well. Makes about 16 biscuits.

GARLIC TOAST

The easy way to enjoy garlic toast.

Thick French bread slices	4-8	4-8
Butter or margarine, softened		
Garlic salt or powder		

Arrange bread on baking sheet. Broil until browned. Turn bread.

Butter untoasted side. Sprinkle with garlic salt. Rub knife over top to press garlic salt into butter. Broil until bubbly and toasted. Serves 4.

DIPPED FRUIT

Makes a light dessert. Simply scrumptious.

FRUIT DIP

Cream cheese, softened	8 oz.	250 mL
Marshmallow cream	¹/₂ cup	125 mL
Frozen concentrated orange juice	2 tsp.	10 mL
Grated orange rind	1 tsp.	5 mL

Sliced apples
Orange segments
Sliced kiwifruit
Seedless grapes
Sliced banana
Cantaloupe cut in balls or pieces
Honeydew cut in balls or pieces.
Blueberries
Raspberries
Strawberries

Fruit Dip: Combine first 4 ingredients in mixing bowl. Beat until smooth. Makes 1 cup (250 mL).

Place assorted fruit on platter with fruit dip in center or divide fruit among 6 plates and pass dip. Serves 4 to 6.

Pictured on page 17.

BLUEBERRY SOUFFLÉ

A wonderful dessert. The soft soufflé topping complements the blueberries. Do make this a "must-try".

Blueberries, fresh or frozen	1 cup	250 mL
Granulated sugar	¹/₃ cup	75 mL
Butter or margarine	3 tbsp.	50 mL
All-purpose flour	6 tbsp.	100 mL
Milk	1¹/₄ cups	275 mL
Granulated sugar	3 tbsp.	50 mL
Grated rind of lemon	¹/₂	¹/₂
Juice of lemon	1	1
Egg yolks	3	3
Egg whites, room temperature	3	3

(continued on next page)

Pour blueberries into 2 quart (2.5 L) casserole. Sprinkle with first amount of sugar.

Melt butter in saucepan. Mix in flour. Cook 1 minute.

Add milk stirring until smooth, boiled and thickened.

Add second amount of sugar, rind of half lemon and juice of whole lemon. Mix. Remove from heat.

Briskly stir in egg yolks.

Beat egg whites until stiff. Fold into lemon mixture. Pour over blueberries. Bake in 350°F (180°C) oven about 35 to 45 minutes until firm and browned. Serves 4.

CHICKEN SALAD

Toasted almonds make it crunchy. Pineapple makes it fruity. Olives add a touch of tartness. Great combination.

Cooked chicken, cut bite size	3 cups	750 mL
Thinly sliced celery	1 cup	250 mL
Slivered almonds, toasted in 350°F (180°C) oven about 5 minutes	1/2 cup	125 mL
Pineapple chunks, drained and cut smaller	14 oz.	398 mL
Sliced black olives or pimiento olives	1/2 cup	125 mL
DRESSING		
Salad dressing (or mayonnaise)	1 cup	250 mL
Curry powder	1/2 tsp.	2 mL
Vinegar	2 tsp.	10 mL
Milk	2 tbsp.	30 mL
Granulated sugar	1 tsp.	5 mL
Cut up head lettuce, lightly packed, or layers of frilly lettuce	8 cups	1.8 L

Combine first 5 ingredients in large bowl.

Dressing: Mix first 5 ingredients in small bowl.

Place lettuce in large bowl. Pour up to 1/2 dressing over top and toss. Arrange on 4 large plates. Add remaining dressing to chicken mixture and toss. Divide among plates over lettuce. Serves 4.

Pictured on cover.

SHRIMP SALAD

This dressing is excellent but other dressings may be used.

BLUE CHEESE DRESSING

Blue cheese, crumbled, use whitest part	2 tbsp.	30 mL
Salad dressing (or mayonnaise)	1/2 cup	125 mL
Sour cream	1/4 cup	60 mL
Vinegar	1 1/2 tsp.	7 mL
Onion powder	1/4 tsp.	1 mL
Garlic powder	1/4 tsp.	1 mL

SALAD

Crisp lettuce, torn	8 cups	1.8 L
Blue Cheese dressing	1/4 cup	50 mL
Crisp lettuce, torn small	4 cups	1 L
Sliced fresh mushrooms	1/2 lb.	250 g
Cooked tiny shrimp	1/2 lb.	250 g
Blue Cheese dressing	1/4 cup	50 mL

Blue Cheese Dressing: Run all ingredients through blender until smooth.

Salad: Combine first amounts of lettuce and dressing in large bowl. Toss. Add more dressing as needed. Arrange on 4 large plates.

Place next 4 ingredients in bowl. Add dressing as needed. Toss. Arrange on center of lettuce on plates. Serves 4.

Pictured on page 89.

EXOTIC SOUP

Noone will be able to guess what kind of soup this is because the curry is hard to detect. Good served with or without it.

Condensed cream of asparagus soup	10 oz.	284 mL
Condensed cream of chicken soup	10 oz.	284 mL
Canned beef bouillon	10 oz.	284 mL
Sour cream	1 cup	250 mL
Curry powder	1/4 tsp.	1 mL
Chopped chives for topping		

Run first 5 ingredients through blender. Pour into saucepan. Heat on medium heat until very hot.

Top with a sprinkle of chives. Makes 4 1/2 cups (1 L). Serves 4.

And great snaps they are.

Brown sugar, packed	1 cup	250 mL
Butter or margarine	1 cup	250 mL
Molasses	1 cup	250 mL
All-purpose flour	4¼ cups	1 L
Ginger	1 tbsp.	15 mL
Salt	1 tsp.	5 mL
Baking soda	1 tsp.	5 mL
Hot water	2 tbsp.	30 mL
Vinegar	1 tbsp.	15 mL
Egg	1	1
Granulated sugar		

Measure brown sugar, butter and molasses into large saucepan. Stir and bring to a boil. Remove from heat and cool.

Add flour, ginger and salt. Stir well.

Dissolve baking soda in hot water. Add to dough along with vinegar and egg, mixing until blended. Roll into 1 inch (2.5 cm) balls.

Roll balls in granulated sugar. Arrange on greased baking sheet. Bake in 300°F (150°C) oven for about 15 minutes. Freezes well. Makes about 6 dozen.

This bread browns on both sides when toasted in the oven.

Butter or margarine, softened	⅓ cup	75 mL
Grated Parmesan cheese	1⅓ tbsp.	20 mL
French bread slices, cut 1 inch (2.5 cm) thick	4-8	4-8

Mix butter and cheese until smooth.

Arrange bread slices on ungreased baking sheet. Spread with cheese mixture. Cook in 400°F (200°C) oven until toasted about 10 minutes. Serves 4 people 1 to 2 slices each.

Pictured on page 125.

VEGETABLE SOUP

Chock full of vegetables.

Diced or cubed potatoes	2 cups	500 mL
Chopped onion	1 cup	250 mL
Chopped cabbage, packed	1 cup	250 mL
Thinly sliced carrot	1/2 cup	125 mL
Diced turnip	1/4 cup	50 mL
Diced parsnip	1/4 cup	50 mL
Water	2 cups	500 mL
Parsley flakes	2 tsp.	10 mL
Vegetable juice (such as V8)	2 cups	500 mL
Salt	1 tsp.	5 mL
Pepper	1/4 tsp.	1 mL

Combine first 8 ingredients in saucepan over medium heat. Bring to a boil. Simmer covered until vegetables are tender about 30 minutes.

Add vegetable juice, salt and pepper. Heat through. Test for seasoning. Freezes well. Serves 4.

Pictured on page 125.

PARMESAN SALAD

Spinach salad dressed with a Parmesan dressing. Creamy good.

PARMESAN DRESSING

Salad dressing (or mayonnaise)	1/3 cup	75 mL
Grated Parmesan cheese	3 tbsp.	50 mL
Lemon juice	2 tsp.	10 mL
Parsley flakes	1/2 tsp.	2 mL
Basil	1/4 tsp.	1 mL
Milk	4 tsp.	20 mL

SALAD

Spinach leaves or romaine lettuce, cut or torn bite size, lightly packed	5 cups	1.12 L
Green onion, thinly sliced	1	1
Peeled, diced cucumber	1/2 cup	125 mL

Parmesan Dressing: Combine all 6 ingredients in small bowl.

Salad: Place spinach or romaine lettuce, onion and cucumber in large bowl. Add dressing and toss. Serves 4.

Elegant! Lots of shrimp.

Cream cheese, softened	4 oz.	125 g
Ripe avocado, peeled and mashed	1	1
Lemon juice	1 tsp.	5 mL
Salt	1/4 tsp.	1 mL
Pepper, light sprinkle		
Garlic powder	1/8 tsp.	0.5 mL
Salad dressing (or mayonnaise)	1/2 cup	125 mL
Milk	2 tbsp.	30 mL
Lemon juice	2 tsp.	10 mL
Dill weed	1/4 tsp.	1 mL
Cooked baby shrimp	1 lb.	454 g
Bread slices, toasted and buttered	8	8
Shredded lettuce, lightly packed	2 cups	500 mL
Cherry tomatoes, halved	4	4
Sprigs of dill for garnish	4	4

Beat first 6 ingredients together in bowl until smooth. Set aside.

In medium size bowl combine salad dressing, milk, lemon juice and dill weed.

Fold in shrimp until coated.

Place 1 slice of toast on each large plate with bottom of slice facing you. Cut remaining slices in half diagonally. Place cut side butting up against both sides of toast on plate.

Spread center slices with lettuce. Spoon avocado mixture over lettuce leaving edges showing.

Divide shrimp over avocado.

Place tomato half at top and bottom of plate. Garnish with a sprig of dill. Serves 4.

Paré Pointer

And a musical insect is a humbug.

CHICKEN SOUP

With chicken in the freezer this simple recipe can be made to enjoy anytime.

Chicken parts, skin removed	1 lb.	500 g
Water	6 cups	1.5 L
Salt	1 tsp.	5 mL
Pepper	1/4 tsp.	1 mL
Bay leaf	1	1
Leeks, white part only	2	2
Medium potatoes, peeled and diced	2	2
Medium carrot, grated	1	1
Chicken bouillon powder	1 tbsp.	15 mL
Parsley flakes	1 tsp.	5 mL

Place chicken parts, water, salt, pepper and bay leaf in large saucepan. Cook covered about 30 minutes until tender. Discard bay leaf. Remove chicken and set liquid aside. Remove meat from bones and chop. Return meat to liquid in saucepan.

Cut leeks in thin slices. Add to soup. Add potato, carrot, bouillon powder and parsley. Simmer covered for 20 to 30 minutes more. Makes 8 cups (1.8 L). Freezes well. Serves 4.

Pictured on cover.

CHICKEN ZUCCHINI SANDWICH

An open faced sandwich with a roasted red pepper sauce.

Large chicken breasts, halved, skin removed	2	2
Water to cover		
Salt	1/2 tsp.	2 mL
PEPPER SAUCE		
Red peppers, roasted and peeled	2	2
Butter or margarine	6 tbsp.	100 mL
All-purpose flour	2 tbsp.	30 mL
Salt	1/4 tsp.	1 mL
Pepper	1/8 tsp.	0.5 mL
Cayenne pepper	1/8 tsp.	0.5 mL
Milk	1 1/4 cups	275 mL
Butter or margarine		
Medium zucchini with peel, cut in slim fingers	2	2
Bread slices, toasted and buttered	8	8

Cook chicken in water and first amount of salt until tender. Drain. Cool to handle. Pull meat off each half in 1 piece. Keep warm.

Pepper Sauce: Meanwhile cut peppers in half lengthwise. Remove seeds. Broil skin sides about 10 minutes until charred black. Turn and broil until edges are charred black about 10 minutes. Peel and cut up.

Melt first amount of butter in saucepan. Mix in flour, salt, pepper and cayenne pepper. Stir in milk and heat until it boils and thickens. Remove from heat. Add red pepper. Run through blender to smooth. Return to saucepan and keep warm.

Melt second amount of butter in frying pan. Add zucchini. Sauté about 5 minutes.

Arrange 1 whole and 2 half slices of toast on each plate. Cut each breast half into 2 layers. If breasts aren't large you should cook 1 extra to fill space on toast. Arrange 2 layers over each center slice of toast. Spoon pepper sauce over chicken. Spoon zucchini over top. Serves 4.

Pictured on page 35.

APPLE DESSERT CAKE

Topped with a lemon sauce, this looks like a wedge of pie. Very moist.

Egg	1	1
Brown sugar, packed	³/₄ cup	175 mL
All-purpose flour	¹/₂ cup	125 mL
Baking powder	1 tsp.	5 mL
Salt	¹/₄ tsp.	1 mL
Cinnamon	¹/₄ tsp.	1 mL
Peeled and chopped apples	1¹/₂ cups	350 mL
Chopped walnuts	¹/₃ cup	75 mL

Beat egg in mixing bowl until frothy. Mix in brown sugar. Add flour, baking powder, salt and cinnamon. Mix until moistened.

Add apple and walnuts. Mix. Spread in greased 8 inch (20 cm) round layer pan or 9 inch (22 cm) pie plate. Bake in 350°F (180°C) oven for about 30 to 35 minutes or until an inserted toothpick comes out clean. Cut in wedges and pour Lemon Sauce over top. Serves 6.

LEMON SAUCE

Granulated sugar	¹/₃ cup	75 mL
All-purpose flour	4 tsp.	20 mL
Salt	¹/₈ tsp.	0.5 mL
Water	1 cup	225 mL
Lemon juice	2 tbsp.	30 mL
Grated lemon rind	1 tsp.	5 mL

Measure sugar, flour and salt into small saucepan. Stir thoroughly.

Add water and stir well. Add lemon juice and rind. Bring to a boil, stirring. Makes 1 cup (225 mL). Serve over Apple Dessert Cake.

APPLE FREEZE

Make this ice cream in no time. As it freezes you can make Ginger Snaps.

Applesauce	1 cup	250 mL
Granulated sugar	6 tbsp.	100 mL
Grated lemon peel	1 tsp.	5 mL
Cinnamon	¹/₄ tsp.	1 mL
Whipping cream	1 cup	250 mL

(continued on next page)

In small bowl combine applesauce, sugar, lemon peel and cinnamon. Mix well.

Beat cream until stiff. Fold applesauce mixture into cream. Turn into shallow pan and freeze. Scoop into bowls to serve with Ginger Snaps, page 121, or place scoops of ice cream on slices of White Cake, page 82. Serves 4.

APPLE SQUARES

Serve these squares warm and top with ice cream. Layers of oatmeal contain apple filling.

Butter or margarine	¹/₂ cup	125 mL
All-purpose flour	1 cup	250 mL
Rolled oats	1 cup	250 mL
Brown sugar	1 cup	250 mL
Salt	¹/₄ tsp.	1 mL
Cooking apples, peeled and cut up (McIntosh is good)	3 cups	750 mL
Granulated sugar	³/₄ cup	175 mL
Vanilla	1¹/₂ tsp.	7 mL
Cinnamon	¹/₄ tsp.	1 mL
Water	1¹/₄ cups	250 mL
Cornstarch	3 tbsp.	50 mL
Water	¹/₄ cup	60 mL
Ice cream		

Melt butter in medium size saucepan. Remove from heat. Stir in flour, rolled oats, brown sugar and salt. Take just over half of mixture and pack in greased 9 x 9 inch (22 x 22 cm) pan.

Combine apples, granulated sugar, vanilla, cinnamon and first amount of water in another saucepan. Bring to a boil and cook, stirring occasionally, until apples are soft.

Mix cornstarch in remaining water. Stir into boiling apples until it returns to a boil and thickens. Pour over oatmeal crust. Sprinkle with remaining crumbs. Bake in 350°F (180°C) oven for 35 minutes or until browned.

Cut into squares. Serve warm with a scoop of ice cream. Cuts into 9 squares.

MENU ONE

Cozy Dogs   page 133
Waldorf Salad   page 131
Apple Cobbler   page 146
Ice Cream
Coffee   Tea   Milk

MENU TWO

Macaroni And Cheese   page 138
Curry Slaw   page 131
White Toast   page 136
Ice Cream Sandwich   page 140
Coffee   Tea   Milk

MENU THREE

Mock Pizza   page 137
Sesame Tossed Salad   page 140
Pickles
Chocolate Cream Pudding   page 147
Coffee   Tea   Milk

MENU FOUR

Pizza Bread   page 132
Tossed Salad   page 14
Grape Freeze   page 149
Puffed Wheat Cake   page 150
Coffee   Tea   Milk

MENU FIVE

Winning Wieners   page 137
Buttered Noodles   page 133
Quick Fruit Salad   page 138
Brownie Cupcakes   page 135
Ice Cream
Coffee   Tea   Milk

MENU SIX

Pita Lunch   page 134
Applekraut Salad   page 147
Crunchies   page 136
Dill Dip   page 136
Vanilla Pudding   page 149
Coffee   Tea   Milk

MENU SEVEN

Fishburger   page 139
Tartar Sauce   page 139
Garden Toss   page 146
Ice Cream
Peanut Butter Sauce   page 142
Coffee   Tea   Milk

MENU EIGHT

Hamburgers   page 134
Chips   page 145
Crunchies   page 136
Dill Dip   page 136
Pickles
Chocolate Sauced Pudding   page 141
Coffee   Tea   Milk

MENU NINE

Fish And Chips   page 145
Tartar Sauce   page 139
Apple Charlotte   page 148
Coffee   Tea   Milk

A crunchy good salad with raisins and nuts.

Large apples, peeled and diced	2	2
Chopped celery	1/2 cup	125 mL
Raisins or currants	1/4 cup	50 mL
Chopped walnuts	1/3 cup	75 mL
Salad dressing (or mayonnaise)	1/3 cup	75 mL
Milk	1 tbsp.	15 mL

Combine first 4 ingredients in bowl.

Measure salad dressing in cup. Stir in milk. Pour over salad immediately and stir to prevent apple from browning. Serves 4.

The mild touch of curry gives a delicious twist to this coleslaw.

Grated cabbage, packed	3 cups	750 mL
Medium carrot, grated	1	1
DRESSING		
Salad dressing (or mayonnaise)	1/2 cup	125 mL
Granulated sugar	1 1/2 tbsp.	25 mL
Vinegar	1 tbsp.	15 mL
Dry onion flakes	2 tsp.	10 mL
Celery seeds	1/4 tsp.	1 mL
Prepared mustard	1/4 tsp.	1 mL
Curry powder	1/8 tsp.	0.5 mL

Combine cabbage and carrot in medium large bowl. Chill until needed.

Dressing: Mix all 7 ingredients in small bowl. Before serving pour over salad. Stir well. Serves 4.

Paré Pointer

A plane Jane is a lady pilot.

PIZZA BREAD

A quick lunch. Just cut a French loaf in half, spread with pizza makings and bake.

French bread loaf, sliced lengthwise, buttered	1	1
Canned tomato paste	5½ oz.	156 mL
Grated Parmesan cheese	3 tbsp.	50 mL
Basil	½ tsp.	2 mL
Oregano	½ tsp.	2 mL
Garlic powder	¼ tsp.	1 mL
Grated mozzarella cheese	2 cups	500 mL
Sliced pepperoni or other cooked meat	1¼ cups	300 mL
Sliced fresh mushrooms	2 cups	500 mL
Small green pepper, diced	1	1
Grated mozarella cheese	1 cup	250 mL
Grated medium Cheddar cheese	½ cup	125 mL

Arrange bread on tray buttered side up. Broil until toasty brown.

Mix next 5 ingredients in small bowl. Spread over bread.

Sprinkle with first amount of mozzarella cheese followed by pepperoni, mushrooms and green pepper. Place on baking tray.

Scatter lengthwise remaining mozzarella cheese over top. Sprinkle Cheddar cheese down center of each bread half. Bake in 450°F (230°C) oven until hot and cheese is melted. Cut each bread half crosswise into 2 to 3 inch (5 to 8 cm) strips. Serves 4.

Pictured on cover.

Parents want their children to reach automatic drive without becoming shiftless.

Simple noodles buttered and parslied.

Medium egg noodles	8 oz.	250 g
Boiling water	2¹/₂ qts.	3 L
Cooking oil	1 tbsp.	15 mL
Salt	2 tsp.	10 mL
Butter or margarine	2 tbsp.	30 mL
Parsley flakes	1 tsp.	5 mL

Cook noodles in boiling water, cooking oil and salt in large uncovered saucepan until tender but firm, about 5 to 7 minutes. Drain. Return noodles to saucepan.

Add butter and parsley. Toss and serve immediately. Serves 4.

COZY DOGS

A tasty tang to these dogs.

Tea biscuit mix	2 cups	500 mL
Cold water	¹/₂ cup	125 mL
Prepared mustard (optional)	4 tsp.	20 mL
Grated medium Cheddar cheese	1 cup	250 mL
Wieners	8	8

Mix biscuit mix and water to form a soft ball. Roll ¹/₈ inch (3 mm) thick on lightly floured surface. Cut into portions a bit longer than wiener and big enough to roll to completely enclose wiener.

Spread biscuit dough lightly with mustard. Sprinkle each with 2 tbsp. (30 mL) cheese. Lay wiener near edge. Roll and seal seam as well as ends. Arrange on ungreased baking sheet. Bake in 425°F (220°C) oven about 15 minutes until browned. Makes 8.

Paré Pointer

When you attend diet clubs it is a losing proposition.

PITA LUNCH

This meaty sandwich uses leftover roast beef. A hearty lunch.

Thinly sliced lettuce, lightly packed	4½ cups	1 L
Cooked roast beef, shaved or chopped	3 cups	700 mL
Grated medium Cheddar cheese	1½ cups	350 mL
Diced tomatoes	1½ cups	350 mL
Salad dressing (or mayonnaise)	6 tbsp.	100 mL
Horseradish	¾ tsp.	4 mL
Prepared mustard	¾ tsp.	4 mL
Onion powder	¼ tsp.	1 mL
Salt, sprinkle		
Pepper, sprinkle		
Pita bread, halved crosswise	4	4

Place lettuce, beef, cheese and tomato in bowl. Add more cheese if desired.

Mix salad dressing, horseradish, mustard, onion powder, salt and pepper in small bowl. Pour over meat mixture. Toss.

Gently open pita along cut side. Divide filling among 8 pita halves. Serves 4.

HAMBURGERS

Good anytime. For a special treat add fried bacon to each burger.

Butter or margarine	2 tbsp.	30 mL
Finely chopped onion	¾ cup	175 mL
Ground beef	1½ lbs.	700 g
Dry bread crumbs	½ cup	125 mL
Water	¼ cup	50 mL
Salt	1½ tsp.	7 mL
Pepper	¼ tsp.	1 mL
Cooking oil	1 tbsp.	15 mL
Hamburger buns, split and buttered	8	8
Lettuce leaves	8	8
Tomato slices	8	8

(continued on next page)

Melt butter in frying pan. Add onion and sauté until soft and tender. Transfer to bowl.

Add ground beef, bread crumbs, water, salt and pepper. Mix. Shape into 8 patties.

Heat cooking oil in frying pan. Cook meat patties until well done, browning both sides.

Insert patty into hamburger bun. Add lettuce and tomato slice. Have the usual condiments on hand such as relish, ketchup, cheese, pickles, etc. Makes 8 to serve 4.

Pictured on page 143.

BROWNIE CUPCAKES

A favorite to eat out of your hand. Ice cream can always be added for a bigger dessert. Freezes well before being iced.

Squares of semisweet baking chocolate	2 × 1 oz.	2 × 28 g
Butter or margarine	1/2 cup	125 mL
Brown sugar, packed	1 1/2 cups	350 mL
All-purpose flour	1 cup	250 mL
Eggs, beaten lightly	2	2
Vanilla	1 tsp.	5 mL
Chopped pecans or walnuts	1/2 cup	125 mL
Salt	1/4 tsp.	1 mL

Melt chocolate and butter in large saucepan over low heat. Stir often to hasten melting. Remove from heat.

Add remaining ingredients. Stir just enough to moisten. Spoon into muffin cups lined with large size paper cups or spoon directly into greased muffin cups filling half full. Bake in 350°F (180°C) oven for 20 to 25 minutes or until an inserted toothpick comes out clean. Serve plain or cool and frost. Makes about 12.

CHOCOLATE ICING

Butter or margarine, softened	3 tbsp.	50 mL
Icing (confectioner's) sugar	1 1/2 cups	375 mL
Cocoa	1/3 cup	75 mL
Water, milk or coffee	2 tbsp.	30 mL

Beat all 4 ingredients together adding more icing sugar or water as needed for each spreading. Ice Brownie Cupcakes.

Pictured on page 143.

CRUNCHIES

A selection of nibblies to round out a lunch.

Cherry tomatoes
Carrot sticks
Celery sticks
Cucumber slices
Radishes
Cauliflower florets
Broccoli florets
Canned baby corn, drained
Mushrooms
Green, red and yellow
  pepper strips

Pick your favorites and serve several of each on a tray. Include Dill Dip, below, to make them even better.

DILL DIP		
Salad dressing (or mayonnaise)	$^2/_3$ **cup**	**175 mL**
Sour cream	$^2/_3$ **cup**	**175 mL**
Dry onion flakes	**2 tsp.**	**10 mL**
Dry parsley flakes	**2 tsp.**	**10 mL**
Dill weed	**2 tsp.**	**10 mL**
Paprika	$^1/_4$ **tsp.**	**1 mL**
Celery salt	$^1/_4$ **tsp.**	**1 mL**

Mix all 7 ingredients in small bowl. Serve as a vegetable dip. Makes about $1^1/_2$ cups (350 mL).

Pictured on page 143.

WHITE TOAST

A method from Hong Kong for serving bread.

Square white bread slices,	**8**	**8**
crusts removed		

Arrange bread slices on baking sheet. Place in 300°F (150°C) oven for 5 minutes. Turn and continue cooking for about 2 minutes more. Slices should feel toasted but be fairly white. Slice in half cornerwise. Let everyone butter their own. Serves 4.

Quick and easy. And a real hit!

English muffins, cut in 2 layers	6	6
Tomato sauce	7½ oz.	213 g
Basil	¼ tsp.	1 mL
Oregano	¼ tsp.	1 mL
Onion powder	¼ tsp.	1 mL
Parsley flakes	¼ tsp.	1 mL
Seasoned salt	½ tsp.	2 mL
Grated mozzarella cheese	1 cup	250 mL
Cherry tomatoes, sliced	12	12
Small mushrooms, sliced	12	12
Bite size pieces of pepperoni, ham, bacon or bologna	60	60
Grated mozzarella cheese	⅓ cup	75 mL

Arrange muffin halves on tray.

In small bowl stir next 6 ingredients. Spread over buns.

Layer next 4 ingredients over tomato sauce in order given.

Sprinkle remaining cheese in center of each. Heat under broiler until hot and cheese is melted and bubbly. These may be prepared ahead and frozen before broiling. Serves 4 people 3 small pizzas each.

Pictured on page 143.

WINNING WIENERS

Delicious flavor. Cooked in a tangy sauce.

Ketchup	½ cup	125 mL
Prepared orange juice (or pineapple)	½ cup	125 mL
Worcestershire sauce	½-1 tsp.	2-5 mL
Liquid smoke, regular	¼ tsp.	1 mL
Onion powder	¼ tsp.	1 mL
Wieners	12	12

In frying pan large enough to hold wieners in single layer, measure first 5 ingredients. Add more Worcestershire sauce to taste.

Add wieners. Bring to a boil. Allow to simmer slowly turning wieners occasionally until sauce is very thick and clings to wieners. Serves 4.

MACARONI AND CHEESE

A tasty old-timer. Creamy.

Elbow macaroni	1½ cups	350 mL
Boiling water	2½ qts.	3 L
Cooking oil	1 tbsp.	15 mL
Salt	2 tsp.	10 mL
Butter or margarine	¼ cup	60 mL
Finely chopped onion	3 tbsp.	50 mL
All-purpose flour	3 tbsp.	50 mL
Salt	½ tsp.	2 mL
Pepper	⅛ tsp.	0.5 mL
Milk	1⅔ cups	375 mL
Steak sauce	½ tsp.	2 mL
Prepared mustard	½ tsp.	2 mL
Grated medium Cheddar cheese, lightly packed	1½ cups	350 mL

In large uncovered saucepan cook macaroni about 5 to 7 minutes, in boiling water, cooking oil and first amount of salt, until tender but firm. Drain.

Melt butter in large saucepan. Add onion and sauté until soft.

Mix in flour, second amount of salt and pepper. Stir in milk until it boils and thickens.

Add steak sauce, mustard and cheese. Stir to melt cheese. Stir in macaroni. Turn into 2 quart (2.5 L) casserole. Cook uncovered in 350°F (180°C) oven for about 30 minutes until bubbly hot. Serves 4.

QUICK FRUIT SALAD

Colorful and delicious. Not too sweet. Just right.

Canned fruit cocktail, drained	14 oz.	398 mL
Tiny marshmallows	2½ cups	625 mL
Chopped walnuts	¼ cup	50 mL
Sour cream	1 cup	250 mL
Lettuce leaves	4	4
Maraschino cherries	4	4

Mix first 4 ingredients in bowl. Let stand at least 1 hour.

Place lettuce leaves on 4 plates. Spoon salad in 4 mounds on lettuce. Top with cherry. Serves 4.

These are fried in a pan rather than a deep-fryer. Made from canned salmon.

Butter or margarine	2 tsp.	10 mL
Chopped onion	1/3 cup	75 mL
Canned salmon with juice, skin and round bones removed	7 1/2 oz.	213 g
Egg	1	1
Dry bread crumbs	1 1/2 cups	350 mL
Prepared mustard	1/2 tsp.	2 mL
Parsley flakes	1/4 tsp.	1 mL
Salt	1/4 tsp.	1 mL
Pepper, sprinkle		
Cornflake crumbs	1/4 cup	50 mL
Butter or margarine	2 tbsp.	30 mL
TARTAR SAUCE		
Salad dressing (or mayonnaise)	2 tbsp.	30 mL
Sweet pickle relish	1 tsp.	5 mL
Hamburger buns, split and buttered	6	6

Melt first amount of butter in saucepan. Add onion and sauté until soft and clear. Remove from heat.

Mix in next 7 ingredients. Shape into 6 patties. If too dry, add another egg.

Dip patties in cornflake crumbs. Melt second amount of butter in frying pan. Add fish patties. Brown both sides.

Tartar Sauce: Stir salad dressing and pickle relish together.

Spread tartar sauce over buttered buns. Insert fish patties. Makes 6.

Pictured on page 143.

Tanning oil can only be used on Sun-days.

SESAME TOSSED SALAD

Bound to be good with sesame seeds added.

Chopped or torn crisp lettuce, lightly packed	5 cups	1.12 L
Green onions, sliced	2	2
Sliced celery	1/2 cup	125 mL
Toasted sesame seeds	3 tbsp.	50 mL
DRESSING		
Cooking oil	1 tbsp.	15 mL
Vinegar	1 tbsp.	15 mL
Granulated sugar	1 tbsp.	15 mL
Prepared mustard	1/4 tsp.	1 mL

Combine lettuce, onion, celery and sesame seeds in bowl. Sesame seeds can be toasted in 350°F (180°C) oven for about 5 to 10 minutes stirring once or twice until lightly browned. Chill salad until needed.

Dressing: Stir all 4 ingredients together until sugar is dissolved. Just before serving pour over salad. Toss. Serves 4.

ICE CREAM SANDWICH

Pink ice cream on a nutty crust, finished off with a chocolate sauce.

CRUMB CRUST		
Butter or margarine	1/2 cup	125 mL
Brown sugar, packed	1/4 cup	60 mL
All-purpose flour	1 cup	250 mL
Chopped walnuts	1/3 cup	75 mL
FILLING		
Strawberry ice cream (rectangular carton)	1 qt.	1 L
CHOCOLATE TOPPING		
Semisweet chocolate chips	1 cup	250 mL
Vanilla	1 tsp.	5 mL
Icing (confectioner's sugar)	1/2 cup	125 mL
Corn syrup	1/4 cup	60 mL
Milk	1/2 cup	125 mL

(continued on next page)

Crumb Crust: Melt butter in saucepan. Stir in sugar, flour and walnuts. Spread on baking sheet. Bake in 350°F (180°C) oven for about 15 minutes, stirring once or twice to ensure even browning. Cool. Spread two-thirds of crumbs on bottom of 8 x 8 inch (20 x 20 cm) pan.

Filling: Lay slices of ice cream over crumbs. Ice cream slices should be at least 1 inch (2.5 cm) thick. Sprinkle with remaining crumbs. Freeze.

Chocolate Topping: Melt chocolate chips in heavy saucepan over low heat. Stir to hasten melting. Add vanilla, icing sugar, corn syrup and milk. Beat with spoon. Serve hot over square of ice cream sandwich. Cuts into 9 squares.

CHOCOLATE SAUCED PUDDING

Bake this all together. When cooked there is sauce under the cake topping to spoon over all.

All-purpose flour	³/₄ cup	175 mL
Granulated sugar	²/₃ cup	150 mL
Cocoa	1¹/₂ tbsp.	25 mL
Baking powder	1¹/₂ tsp.	7 mL
Salt	¹/₄ tsp.	1 mL
Milk	¹/₃ cup	75 mL
Butter or margarine, softened	1¹/₂ tbsp.	25 mL
Vanilla	1 tsp.	5 mL
Brown sugar, packed	³/₄ cup	175 mL
Cocoa	3 tbsp.	50 mL
Hot water	1¹/₃ cups	300 mL

Measure first 5 ingredients into bowl. Stir.

Add milk, butter and vanilla. Mix well. Turn into 2 quart (2.5 L) casserole. Smooth top.

Stir brown sugar and second amount of cocoa together. Sprinkle over batter in casserole.

Slowly pour hot water over all. Do not stir. Bake in 350°F (180°C) oven for about 40 minutes. Serves 4 generously.

PEANUT BUTTER SAUCE

A treat for ice cream.

Granulated sugar	1 cup	250 mL
All-purpose flour	¼ cup	60 mL
Milk	¾ cup	175 mL
Smooth peanut butter	⅓ cup	75 mL
Corn syrup	1 tbsp.	15 mL
Ice cream scoops	4	4

Measure sugar and flour into saucepan. Stir well.

Add next 3 ingredients. Mix thoroughly. Place over medium heat stirring until boiling. Remove from heat. Cool.

Place ice cream scoops in dishes. Spoon sauce over top. Makes 1½ cups (350 mL) sauce.

Fish is dipped in egg and coated with crumbs. It produces an appetizing rich brown color.

Fish fillets, fairly thin, sole or cod	1³/₄ lbs.	800 g
Eggs, beaten	2	2
Fine dry breadcrumbs	¹/₂ cup	125 mL
Fat for deep-frying		

Cut fish fillets into easy to handle pieces. Pat dry with paper towels.

Dip fish in egg and coat with crumbs. Beat another egg if needed.

Drop into hot fat 375°F (180°C) about 3 minutes to cook and brown both sides. Keep hot in 325°F (160°C) oven until all is deep-fried. Serve with Tartar Sauce, page 139, and wedges of lemon. Serves 4.

CHIPS

Old potatoes, peeled	4-5	4-5
Cold water		
Fat for deep-frying		
Salt, sprinkle		

Cut potatoes lengthwise in slices about ¹/₃ inch (1 cm) thick. Cut each slice into strips about ¹/₃ inch (1 cm) wide. Cover with cold water in large container. Let stand for 1 hour. Drain well. Pat dry with a cloth.

Place some potato strips into wire basket. Lower into hot fat 375°F (190°C) and cook about 6 minutes until golden and tender. Drain on paper towels.

Sprinkle with salt. Serves 4.

Pictured on page 143.

Plumbers probably have many pipe dreams.

APPLE COBBLER

The aroma from this will make everyone want their dessert first.

Cooking apples, peeled and sliced	4 cups	1 L
Brown sugar, packed	½ cup	125 mL
Cinnamon, sprinkle		
Water	⅓ cup	75 mL
TOPPING		
All-purpose flour	1½ cups	350 mL
Granulated sugar	2 tbsp.	30 mL
Baking powder	1 tbsp.	15 mL
Salt	½ tsp.	2 mL
Butter or margarine	¼ cup	60 mL
Egg, beaten	1	1
Milk	6 tbsp.	100 mL
Granulated sugar, sprinkle		

Pile apples in 2 quart (2.5 L) casserole. Spread brown sugar over top. Sprinkle with cinnamon. Add water. Cover and bake in 350°F (180°C) oven about 30 minutes until soft.

Topping: Measure first 5 ingredients into bowl. Stir.

Add egg and milk. Stir to moisten. Drop by small spoonfuls over apples. Turn oven to 425°F (220°C).

Sprinkle with sugar. Bake uncovered for about 20 minutes until risen and browned. Serves 4.

GARDEN TOSS

Any time of year salad. Contains crunchy sunflower seeds.

Lettuce, cut up and lightly packed	4 cups	1 L
Radishes, sliced	8	8
Medium carrots, grated	1-2	1-2
Sunflower seeds	2 tbsp.	30 mL
Italian dressing	¼ cup	50 mL

Combine lettuce, radish, carrot and sunflower seeds in large bowl. Chill.

When ready to serve, add dressing. Toss well. Serves 4.

Try this for something different in a salad .

Sauerkraut, drained	1¹/₂ cups	375 mL
Chopped celery	¹/₂ cup	125 mL
Chopped onion	¹/₃ cup	75 mL
Large apple, peeled and diced	1	1
Chopped green pepper	¹/₄ cup	50 mL
Chopped red pepper	¹/₄ cup	50 mL
Granulated sugar	¹/₂ cup	125 mL
Vinegar	¹/₄ cup	50 mL

Place first 6 ingredients in bowl.

Heat sugar and vinegar in small saucepan until sugar is dissolved. Cool. Pour over salad. Mix. Let stand overnight. Serves 4.

Pictured on page 89.

CHOCOLATE CREAM PUDDING

An easy, from-the-shelf dessert.

Envelope of dessert topping	1	1
Milk as package directs	¹/₂ cup	110 mL
Semisweet chocolate chips, melted and cooled	¹/₃ cup	75 mL
Instant chocolate pudding, 4 serving size	1	1
Milk	2 cups	450 mL

Combine dessert topping, first amount of milk and melted chocolate chips in small mixing bowl. Beat until stiff. Reserve ¹/₄ cup (50 mL) for topping.

Add pudding mix and remaining milk. Mix, then beat on high speed for 2 minutes. Pour into sherbets or fruit nappies. Top with a dab of reserved cream. Serves 4 very generously.

Paré Pointer

Point out two physicians and you see a paradox.

APPLE CHARLOTTE

When this dessert is unmolded it reveals heart cut-outs of bread on top. Lots of eye appeal.

White bread slices, crust removed	3	3
White bread slices for hearts	3	3
Cooking apples, peeled, thinly sliced	4	4
Granulated sugar	$\frac{1}{2}$ cup	125 mL
Cinnamon	$1\frac{1}{2}$ tsp.	7 mL
Butter or margarine	2 tbsp.	30 mL
Moist bread crumbs made from crustless slices (about 4)	2 cups	500 mL
SAUCE		
Apricot jam	$\frac{1}{2}$ cup	125 mL
Apple juice, apricot nectar or orange juice	$\frac{1}{4}$ cup	50 mL

Grease straight sided 1 quart ($1\frac{1}{2}$ L) casserole. Cut 3 slices crustless bread in half. Line sides of casserole. With heart shaped cookie cutter cut 5 hearts about $2\frac{3}{8}$ inches (6 cm) wide, 2 per slice, to line bottom of casserole.

Mix sugar and cinnamon in small bowl.

Assemble layers in casserole as follows:

1. Slices of 1 apple
2. 2 tbsp. (30 mL) sugar-cinnamon mixture
3. Dab with pieces of $\frac{1}{2}$ tbsp. butter
4. $\frac{1}{2}$ cup (125 mL) bread crumbs

Repeat 3 more times. Bake in 350°F (180°C) oven about 1 hour to 1 hour 15 minutes until apples are tender. Let stand on rack for 10 minutes. Carefully loosen around edge of casserole with knife. Hold plate over top and turn over to unmold onto plate. Serve warm.

Sauce: While pudding is cooking, stir jam and fruit juice together in small saucepan. Warm sauce. Dish up pudding and top with a bit of sauce. Serves 4.

Make a milk pudding from scratch.

Milk	3 cups	700 mL
Granulated sugar	3/4 cup	175 mL
All-purpose flour	6 tbsp.	100 mL
Salt	1/2 tsp.	2 mL
Eggs	2	2
Vanilla	1 1/2 tsp.	7 mL
Raspberry, blackberry or black currant jelly, or raspberries or strawberries with juice (optional)		

Heat milk in heavy saucepan until it boils.

Measure sugar, flour and salt into bowl. Stir.

Add eggs and vanilla. Beat together with spoon. Stir into boiling milk until it returns to a boil and thickens. Pour into bowl. If you plan to serve cold, cover top of pudding with plastic wrap. Be sure plastic touches pudding to prevent a crust from forming.

Top with jelly or leave plain. Pouring cream and whipped cream make good toppings also. Serves 4.

Easy enough for the young cooks to make on their own.

Grape flavored gelatin	3 oz.	85 g
Granulated sugar	1/4 cup	50 mL
Boiling water	1 cup	225 mL
Cold water	1 cup	225 mL
Whipping cream (or 1 envelope topping)	1 cup	250 mL

Dissolve gelatin and sugar in boiling water in medium size bowl.

Stir in cold water. Chill until syrupy.

Beat cream in small mixing bowl until stiff. Fold into gelatin. Spoon into plastic cartons and freeze. Serves 4.

PUFFED WHEAT CAKE

A chocolate confection that can be eaten as a snack as well as with ice cream or fruit.

Brown sugar, packed	1 cup	250 mL
Honey	½ cup	125 mL
Margarine	½ cup	125 mL
Cocoa	2 tbsp.	30 mL
Vanilla	½ tsp.	2 mL
Puffed wheat	6 cups	1.5 L
Crisp rice cereal	2 cups	500 mL

Combine first 4 ingredients in heavy saucepan. Stir often as you bring mixture to a boil. Boil about 5 to 8 minutes until a small spoonful forms a soft ball in cold water or temperature reaches soft ball stage on candy thermometer.

Remove from heat and stir in vanilla.

Place puffed wheat and rice cereal in large greased bowl. Pour hot mixture over cereal. Stir to coat. Pack into greased 9 x 9 inch (22 x 22 cm) pan.

Pictured on page 143.

Pare Pointer

Coffee is better known as break fluid.

Throughout this book measurements are given in Imperial and Metric measure. To compensate for differences between the two measurements due to rounding, a full metric measure is not always used.

The cup used is the standard 8 fluid ounce. Temperature is given in degrees Fahrenheit and Celsius. Baking Pan measurements are in inches and centimetres as well as quarts and litres. An exact conversion is given below as well as the working equivalent (Standard Measure).

IMPERIAL	METRIC Exact Conversion	Standard Measure
Spoons	millilitre (mL)	millilitre (mL)
$1/4$ teaspoon (tsp.)	1.2 mL	1 mL
$1/2$ teaspoon (tsp.)	2.4 mL	2 mL
1 teaspoon (tsp.)	4.7 mL	5 mL
2 teaspoons (tsp.)	9.4 mL	10 mL
1 tablespoon (tbsp.)	14.2 mL	15 mL
Cups		
$1/4$ cup (4 tbsp.)	56.8 mL	50 mL
$1/3$ cup ($5^1/3$ tbsp.)	75.6 mL	75 mL
$1/2$ cup (8 tbsp.)	113.7 mL	125 mL
$2/3$ cup ($10^2/3$ tbsp.)	151.2 mL	150 mL
$3/4$ cup (12 tbsp.)	170.5 mL	175 mL
1 cup (16 tbsp.)	227.3 mL	250 mL
$4^1/2$ cups	984.8 mL	1000 mL, 1 litre (1 L)
Ounces (oz.)	**Grams (g)**	**Grams (g)**
1 oz.	28.3 g	30 g
2 oz.	56.7 g	55 g
3 oz.	85.0 g	85 g
4 oz.	113.4 g	125 g
5 oz.	141.7 g	140 g
6 oz.	170.1 g	170 g
7 oz.	198.4 g	200 g
8 oz.	226.8 g	250 g
16 oz.	453.6 g	500 g
32 oz.	917.2 g	1000 g, 1 kilogram (1 kg)

PANS, CASSEROLES

Imperial	Metric	Imperial	Metric
8x8 inch	20x20 cm	$1^2/3$ qt.	2 L
9x9 inch	22x22 cm	2 qt..	2.5 L
9x13 inch	22x33 cm	$3^1/3$ qt.	4 L
10x15 inch	25x38 cm	1 qt.	1.2 L
11x17 inch	28x43 cm	$1^1/4$ qt.	1.5 L
8x2 inch round	20x5 cm	$1^2/3$ qt.	2 L
9x2 inch round	22x5 cm	2 qt.	2.5 L
10x4½ inch tube	25x11 cm	$4^1/4$ qt.	5 L
8x4x3 inch loaf	20x10x7 cm	$1^1/4$ qt.	1.5 L
9x5x3 inch loaf	23x12x7 cm	$1^2/3$ qt.	2 L

OVEN TEMPERATURES

Fahrenheit (°F)	Celsius (°C)
175°	80°
200°	100°
225°	110°
250°	120°
275°	140°
300°	150°
325°	160°
350°	180°
375°	190°
400°	200°
425°	220°
450°	230°
475°	240°
500°	260°

INDEX

154

COOKBOOKS

COMPANY'S COMING
PUBLISHING LIMITED
BOX 8037, STATION "F"
EDMONTON, ALBERTA,
CANADA T6H 4N9

SAVE $5.00 *Order any 2 cookbooks by mail at regular prices and SAVE $5.00 on every third cookbook per order.*

ENGLISH TITLE (Hard Cover @ $17.95 each)	QUANTITY	AMOUNT
JEAN PARÉ'S FAVORITES VOLUME ONE - 232 pages		
TITLE (Soft Cover @ $10.95 each)		
150 DELICIOUS SQUARES		
CASSEROLES		
MUFFINS & MORE		
SALADS		
APPETIZERS		
DESSERTS		
SOUPS & SANDWICHES		
HOLIDAY ENTERTAINING		
COOKIES		
VEGETABLES		
MAIN COURSES		
PASTA		
CAKES		
BARBECUES		
DINNERS OF THE WORLD		
LUNCHES		
PIES (September, 1992)		
TOTAL ENGLISH BOOKS (Carry total to next column)		$

FRENCH TITLE (Soft Cover @ $10.95 each)	QUANTITY	AMOUNT
150 DÉLICIEUX CARRÉS		
LES CASSEROLES		
MUFFINS ET PLUS		
LES DÎNERS		
LES BARBECUES (May, 1992)		
LES TARTES (September, 1992)		
DÉLICES DES FÊTES (October, 1992)		
TOTAL FRENCH BOOKS		
TOTAL COST OF FRENCH BOOKS		$
TOTAL COST OF ENGLISH BOOKS		$
TOTAL COST OF ALL BOOKS		$
LESS $5.00 for every third book per order		–
PLUS $1.50 postage & handling **PER BOOK**		+
SUB TOTAL		$
Canadian residents add GST #R101075620		+
TOTAL AMOUNT ENCLOSED		$

Please send the above cookbooks to the address on the reverse side of this coupon.

■ *Prices subject to change without prior notice.*   ■ *Sorry, no C.O.D.'s*

ORDERS OUTSIDE CANADA: *Must be paid in U.S. funds by cheque or money order drawn on Canadian or U.S. bank.*

MAKE CHEQUE OR MONEY ORDER PAYABLE TO: *COMPANY'S COMING PUBLISHING LIMITED*

▼   GIFT CARD MESSAGE   ▼

A GIFT FOR YOU

COOKBOOKS

A NATIONAL BEST SELLER

I would like to order the Company's Coming Cookbooks listed on the reverse side of this coupon.

NAME_____
(PLEASE PRINT)

STREET_____

CITY _____

PROVINCE/STATE _____ POSTAL CODE/ZIP _____

GIFT GIVING – WE MAKE IT EASY...
... YOU MAKE IT DELICIOUS!

Let us help you with your gift giving! We will send cookbooks directly to the recipients of your choice if you give us their names and addresses. Be sure to specify the titles of the cookbooks you wish to send to each person.

Enclose a personal note or card for each gift or use our handy gift card below.

Company's Coming Cookbooks are the perfect gift for birthdays, showers, Mother's Day, Father's Day, graduation or any occasion ... collect them all!

Don't forget to take advantage of the **$5.00 saving ... buy any two Company's Coming Cookbooks by mail and save $5.00 on every third copy per order.**

↓ GIFT CARD MESSAGE ↓

COOKBOOKS

COMPANY'S COMING
PUBLISHING LIMITED
BOX 8037, STATION "F"
EDMONTON, ALBERTA,
CANADA T6H 4N9

SAVE $5.00!

SAVE $5.00 *Order any 2 cookbooks by mail at regular prices and SAVE $5.00 on every third cookbook per order.*

ENGLISH			FRENCH		
TITLE (Hard Cover @ $17.95 each)	QUANTITY	AMOUNT	TITLE (Soft Cover @ $10.95 each)	QUANTITY	AMOUNT
JEAN PARÉ'S FAVORITES VOLUME ONE - 232 pages			150 DÉLICIEUX CARRÉS		
			LES CASSEROLES		
TITLE (Soft Cover @ $10.95 each)			MUFFINS ET PLUS		
150 DELICIOUS SQUARES			LES DÎNERS		
CASSEROLES			LES BARBECUES (May, 1992)		
MUFFINS & MORE			LES TARTES (September, 1992)		
SALADS			DÉLICES DES FÊTES (October, 1992)		
APPETIZERS			**TOTAL FRENCH BOOKS**		
DESSERTS					
SOUPS & SANDWICHES					
HOLIDAY ENTERTAINING					
COOKIES					
VEGETABLES			TOTAL COST OF FRENCH BOOKS		$
MAIN COURSES			TOTAL COST OF ENGLISH BOOKS		$
PASTA			TOTAL COST OF ALL BOOKS		$
CAKES			LESS $5.00 for every third book per order		–
BARBECUES					
DINNERS OF THE WORLD			PLUS $1.50 postage & handling **PER BOOK**		+
LUNCHES			SUB TOTAL		$
PIES (September, 1992)			Canadian residents add GST #R101075620		+
TOTAL ENGLISH BOOKS (Carry total to next column)		$	**TOTAL AMOUNT ENCLOSED**		$

Please send the above cookbooks to the address on the reverse side of this coupon.

■ *Prices subject to change without prior notice.*   ■ *Sorry, no C.O.D.'s*

ORDERS OUTSIDE CANADA: *Must be paid in U.S. funds by cheque or money order drawn on Canadian or U.S. bank.*

MAKE CHEQUE OR MONEY ORDER PAYABLE TO: *COMPANY'S COMING PUBLISHING LIMITED*

▼   GIFT CARD MESSAGE   ▼

COOKBOOKS

A GIFT FOR YOU

COOKBOOKS

A NATIONAL BEST SELLER

I would like to order the Company's Coming Cookbooks listed on the reverse side of this coupon.

NAME_____
(PLEASE PRINT)

STREET_____

CITY _____

PROVINCE/STATE _____ POSTAL CODE/ZIP _____

GIFT GIVING – WE MAKE IT EASY...
... YOU MAKE IT DELICIOUS!

Let us help you with your gift giving! We will send cookbooks directly to the recipients of your choice if you give us their names and addresses. Be sure to specify the titles of the cookbooks you wish to send to each person.

Enclose a personal note or card for each gift or use our handy gift card below.

Company's Coming Cookbooks are the perfect gift for birthdays, showers, Mother's Day, Father's Day, graduation or any occasion ... collect them all!

Don't forget to take advantage of the **$5.00 saving ... buy any two Company's Coming Cookbooks by mail and save $5.00 on every third copy per order.**

↓ GIFT CARD MESSAGE ↓